MESOPOTAMIA

EUPHRATES

ASSYRIA

TIGRIS RIVER

Babylon

RIVER

Ur

N

Old Testament

A BIBLE HISTORY

For Schools, Confirmation Classes and Homes

Prepared by

J. VINCENT NORDGREN

•

Under the Direction of
The Board of Parish Education
of the
Evangelical Lutheran Augustana Synod
of North America

AUGUSTANA BOOK CONCERN · ROCK ISLAND, ILLINOIS

1 9 4 7

Printed in the United States of America

CONTENTS

Part I – THE OLD TESTAMENT

INTRODUCTION

THE BEGINNINGS

THE HISTORY OF THE PATRIARCHS

THE MAKING OF A NATION

Part II – THE NEW TESTAMENT

THE BEGINNING OF THE CHRISTIAN CHURCH

THE OLD TESTAMENT

THE BIBLE

No other book means so much to Christian people as the Bible. This is because this sacred Book speaks to people about the thing that matters most in all the world: their life with God. We call it the Word of God because in it God speaks to us of our deepest needs and our highest hopes. We call it the Book of Life because it shows the way to eternal life and is a guide in Christian living for every generation.

Though the Book is very old, its message is still fresh and full of power. Many different writers have written parts of it. The names of some of them we know, such as David, Samuel, Matthew, Luke, Peter, and Paul. The names of others we do not know, such as the priests and prophets who wrote some parts of the Old Testament and the good man who wrote the Epistle to the Hebrews. Moreover, the different parts of the Bible come from various periods of history. All of the New Testament was written rather soon after the death of Christ, but parts of the Old Testament go back many centuries before the time of Christ and they tell of things that took place far away in the very dim past. We must never forget that these words of eternal life were not originally in one book, but have been collected from many sources and from many periods in history. Throughout this Bible, however, the God of the Ages is always speaking.

Christians believe that God has revealed himself in a special way within the history of mankind. He has done numerous things that show his purpose to redeem man. He has spoken through Moses and the prophets; his judgments can be seen in the course of human history; through the life and death of Jesus Christ He revealed himself in a very special way; and through the Sacred Scriptures we have an unfailing guide which the Holy Spirit continues to use for the faith and conduct of the redeemed.

To be sure, God has also shown us many things about his power and good purposes through the created world about us, but it is through his Word that we have a definite revelation of his good and gracious will to save men from

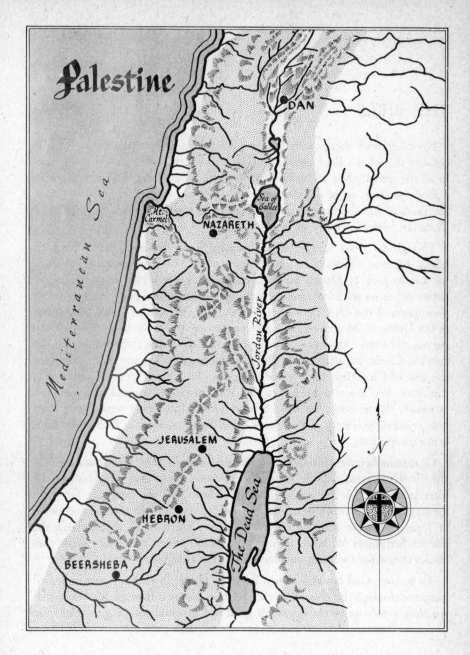

Palestine

DAN

Mediterranean Sea

Mt. Carmel

NAZARETH

Sea of Galilee

Jordan River

JERUSALEM

The Dead Sea

HEBRON

BEERSHEBA

N

sin and death and to give them eternal life. The greatest truths which mankind knows have come from the Bible. It is more than a record of mankind's experience in seeking God; it is primarily the account of what God has done for man.

But if the Bible is to be of value to us who live today, the Book must be read. In our Bible History we have the Bible in shortened form; it is a summary of the main things that are told us in the Book so that we may be helped to know the story it tells and live by the truth and wisdom it teaches.

Our Bible History is divided into two parts: The Old Testament and The New Testament.

The Old Testament tells of the beginnings of the world and of man's need for a Saviour. It also tells a long story of how God chose and trained the Jewish people as the nation in which Christ, the promised Saviour, was to be born.

The New Testament tells of how the promises of the Old Testament were fulfilled when Jesus Christ came into the world to save sinners. It tells also of how this good news was spread among the nations after the resurrection of our Lord.

THE HOLY LAND

Palestine lies to the east of the Mediterranean Sea, with Egypt to the south and Syria to the north and east. The name comes from Philistia, which means the land of the Philistines; these people inhabited its seacoast plains about the time that Moses led his people out of Egypt. Among the Israelites Palestine was called Canaan.

One can think of this important country as divided into four parallel strips or areas. The first is the plain along the seacoast, extending north and south almost the entire length of the country. To the east of this is a strip of mountainous land, which is the backbone of the country and was the principal home of the Israelites. Next is the valley of the Jordan River, which begins in the Lebanon mountains, moves southward into the Sea of Galilee, and from there to the Dead Sea. To the east of the valley is a strip of plateau country, well suited for pasture land. The eastern side of this plateau is bounded by the great Syrian desert.

Palestine is not a large country. From north to south (Dan to Beer-sheba) it is about 130 miles long. From the seacoast on the Mediterranean to the swift-flowing Jordan it is about 30 to 50 miles wide. East of the Jordan the strip of territory belonging to Palestine is about 20 miles wide. The area on both sides of the Jordan is about the size of Switzerland, or the states of Massachusetts and Connecticut combined. But the part that is most famous in history, the western side between the Jordan River and the Mediterranean Sea, is about the same size as Massachusetts alone.

In this small area happened most of the events told in the Old Testament, and they are events which have done much to determine the history of the whole world. To be sure, the empires to the south and east, and later, to the west, were far more extensive. But it is not size that counts. It is what the people do. And in the case of Palestine it was chiefly what the Israelites did in response to the guidance and help of the living God. Palestine is called the Holy Land because of what the Holy One of Israel did with this people, and because of what He did with other nations of the world through this chosen people.

Palestine had no natural ports, but to the north in Phoenicia there were two great harbors: Tyre and Sidon. Their ships sailed far and wide over the Mediterranean Sea. Most of Palestine's relations, however, were with countries reached over caravan trails to the south and east.

To the east lay the ancient empires succeeding one another in power and control over neighbors: Assyria, Babylonia, the Medes and Persians. Out of Babylon, Abraham migrated to Canaan. From Assyria, and later from Babylonia, came armies that were to cause much trouble to Israel and finally destroy its independence.

To the south lay Egypt, whence Israel was led by Moses. Again and again Egypt sought to use Israel as an ally in warfare with the nations to the east. Time after time Palestine was overrun by armies.

In times of peace, Palestine was the corridor through which great merchant caravans passed to carry on their trade north, south, east, and west. So this small country was for many countries the crossroads of the world.

CHAPTER ONE

THE BEGINNINGS

How did the world begin? Where did people come from? Who made them live, and why must they die?

These are questions that man cannot really answer without the help of God. Many answers have been offered to explain the origin of the world, but only the Bible says, "In the beginning God . . ."

Genesis, the first book of the Bible, goes far back into the dim past. It gives us stories that were told by word of mouth in the tents of wandering people and around the camp-fires at night, long before they were written down. Abraham, Isaac, and Jacob each told them in turn to his children, and so they passed from person to person.

These are stories that tell not only how God made the world and all the things that are in it: sun, moon, stars, earth, trees, animals; they also tell the very important story of man and woman: how sin and death came into the world, how Adam and Eve were driven out of Eden, how the great flood swept over the earth, and how the peoples of the earth were scattered.

THE CREATION

In the beginning God created the heaven and the earth. And the earth was without form and void, and darkness was upon the face of the deep; but the Spirit of God moved upon the face of the waters.

And God said, "Let there be light!" And there was light. And God divided the light from the darkness, and called the light Day and the darkness Night. Evening came, and morning, the first day.

And God said, "Let there be a firmament in the midst of the waters, and let it divide the waters from the waters!" And it was so. And God called the firmament Heaven. Evening came, and morning, the second day.

And God said, "Let the waters under the heaven be gathered together unto one place, and let the dry land appear!" And it was so. And God called the dry land Earth, and the gathering together of waters he called Seas. And God said, "Let the earth bring forth grass, the herb yielding seed, and the fruit tree yielding fruit after its kind!" And it was so. Evening came, and morning, the third day.

And God said, "Let there be lights in the firmament of the heaven!" And it was so. And God made a great light to rule the day, and a lesser light to rule the night; he made the stars also. Evening came, and morning, the fourth day.

And God said, "Let the waters bring forth abundantly the moving creatures that have life, and birds that fly above the earth in the heaven!" And it was so. Evening came, and morning, the fifth day.

And God said, "Let the earth bring forth cattle, and creeping things, and beasts of the earth!" And it was so. And God made all manner of living creatures that are upon the earth.

And God said, "Let us make man in our image, after our likeness, and let them have dominion over the fish of the sea, and over the fowl of the air, and over the cattle, and over all the earth!" And the Lord God formed man of the dust of the ground, and breathed into his nostrils the breath of life; and man became a living soul. And God created man in his own image, in the image of God created he him.

And the Lord God said, "It is not good that the man should be alone; I will make a help meet for him." And the Lord God caused a deep sleep to fall upon the man, and while he slept God took one of his ribs. And the Lord God made a woman out of the rib and brought her unto the man. God called the man Adam (that is, "taken from the earth"); and Adam called his wife Eve (which means "mother of life"). And God blessed them and said, "Be fruitful and multiply and fill the earth!"

And God saw everything that he had made, and behold, it was very good. Evening came, and morning, the sixth day.

And on the seventh day God ended his work which he had made; and he rested on the seventh day from all his work which he had made. And God blessed the seventh day and sanctified it, because in it he rested from all his work.

THE FALL

In Eden God planted a garden called Paradise, and out of the ground he made to grow every tree that is pleasant to the sight and good for food. In

After the Fall

21

the midst thereof he placed two trees, one the tree of life, the other the tree of knowledge of good and evil.

And the Lord God put the man into the garden of Eden to tend it and keep it. And the Lord God commanded the man saying, "Of every tree of the garden thou mayest freely eat; but of the tree of the knowledge of good and evil thou shalt not eat, for in the day thou eatest thereof, thou shalt surely die."

Now the serpent was more clever than any beast of the field, and he said to the woman, "Has God said that you are not to eat of every tree of the garden?" The woman answered, "We may eat of the fruit of the trees of the garden; but of the fruit of the tree which is in the midst of the garden God has said: Ye shall not eat of it, neither shall ye touch it, lest ye die." And the serpent said to the woman, "You shall not die; for God knows that in the day you eat from it, then your eyes shall be opened, and you shall be like God, knowing good and evil."

And the woman saw that the tree was good for food, and that it was pleasant to the eyes, and a tree to be desired to make one wise; and she took of the fruit of it, and did eat, and gave also to her husband, and he did eat. Then their eyes were opened, and they knew that they were naked. And they sewed fig leaves together to cover their nakedness.

And they heard the voice of the Lord God in the garden in the cool of the day; and Adam and his wife hid themselves from the presence of the Lord God amongst the trees of the garden. And the Lord God called to Adam and said to him, "Where art thou?" And he said, "I heard thy voice in the garden, and I was afraid, because I was naked; therefore I hid myself." And God said, "Who told thee that thou wast naked? Hast thou eaten of the tree, whereof I commanded thee that thou shouldest not eat?" Adam answered, "The woman whom thou gavest to be with me, she gave me of the tree, and I did eat." And the Lord God said unto the woman, "What is this that thou hast done?" The woman said, "The serpent misled me, and I did eat."

And the Lord God said to the serpent, "Because thou has done this, thou art cursed above all cattle and above every beast of the field! I will put enmity between thee and the woman, and between thy seed and her seed. It shall bruise thy head, and thou shalt bruise his heel."

To the woman he said, "I will greatly multiply thy sorrow; in pain thou shalt bring forth children, and thy husband shall rule over thee."

And unto Adam he said, "Cursed is the ground for thy sake; thorns and thistles shall it bring forth to thee. In the sweat of thy face shalt thou eat bread, till thou return unto the ground; for dust thou art, and unto dust shalt thou return."

And God drove them out of the garden of Eden. At the entrance he placed angels with fiery swords, to guard the way to the tree of life. So God sent Adam forth from the garden to till the ground from whence he was taken.

CAIN AND ABEL

Adam and Eve had several sons and daughters. The oldest sons were Cain and Abel. Cain was a farmer, while Abel was a shepherd. Both offered sacrifices to God: Abel, a lamb; and Cain, some grain from the crops he had raised. God, knowing the secrets of their hearts, was pleased with Abel and his offering, but with Cain and his offering he was not pleased.

When Cain saw this, he became very angry. And God said, "Why art thou angry, and why art thou downcast? Sin is lying in wait at the door, ready to strike thee, but do thou master it."

But when they were in the field, Cain attacked his brother and killed him. The Lord said to Cain, "Where is Abel thy brother?" He said, "I know not. Am I my brother's keeper?" But the Lord said, "What hast thou done? The voice of thy brother's blood crieth unto me from the ground. And now art thou cursed from the earth, which opened its mouth to receive thy brother's blood from thy hand. When thou tillest thy ground, it shall not henceforth yield unto thee its strength. A fugitive and a vagabond shalt thou be on the earth." And Cain said, "My punishment is greater than I can bear." And Cain went out from the presence of the Lord.

After Abel's death Eve gave birth to a son and called him Seth, saying, "God has given me another son instead of Abel."

THE DELUGE

When the Lord saw that the wickedness of man on the earth was great, and that man's mind was never on anything but evil, the Lord regretted that he had ever made man on the earth, and he was grieved in his heart.

So the Lord said, "I will blot him off the earth, both man, and beast, and creeping things, and birds of the heavens; for I regret that I have made them."

But Noah was a just man and walked with God, and he found favor with the Lord. And the Lord said to him, "I have seen thee righteous before me

The Bow in the Cloud

in this generation. Make an ark of gopher wood, build rooms in the ark, and cover it with pitch, inside and outside. The length of it shall be four hundred and fifty feet, the breadth seventy-five feet, and the height forty-five feet. I shall bring a flood of waters upon the earth, to destroy all flesh. But with thee I will establish my covenant, and thou shalt come into the ark, thou, and thy sons, and thy wife, and thy sons' wives. Also, of all living creatures, two of every sort shalt thou bring into the ark, to keep them alive with thee. Take also some of every kind of food for thee and for them." Thus did Noah according to all that God commanded him.

After this Noah and his sons, Shem, Ham, and Japheth, and his wife, and his sons' wives, and all the animals entered into the ark. And all the fountains of the great deep were burst asunder, and the windows of heaven were opened; and the rain came upon the earth forty days and forty nights. And the waters increased for one hundred and fifty days and lifted the ark so that it rose above the earth. The waters rose higher and higher until all mountains were covered. Every living creature upon the earth perished; only Noah and they that were with him in the ark remained alive.

But God remembered Noah and every living thing that was with him in the ark. For a hundred and fifty days the waters covered the earth. Then the sun came out and the waters began to recede. At last the ark touched solid ground. This was in the mountains of Ararat. Then Noah sent out a dove, but the dove soon returned, not finding a place where her foot might rest. After seven days Noah again sent out the dove. In the evening she returned, carrying in her beak an olive leaf. So Noah knew that the flood had ended.

GOD'S COVENANT WITH NOAH

At the command of God, Noah and his wife, and his sons and his sons' wives, and every living creature that was with them came out of the ark. And Noah built an altar to the Lord and offered burnt offerings. And the Lord said, "I will not again curse the ground any more for man's sake. While the earth remaineth, seed time and harvest, and cold and heat, and summer and winter, and day and night shall not cease."

And God blessed Noah and said, "Behold, I establish my covenant with thee; neither shall there any more be a flood to destroy the earth. I set my bow in the cloud; it shall be the sign of a covenant between me and the earth."

THE TOWER OF BABEL

After the deluge man again began to multiply on the earth, but they were all of one language.

In their pride, they decided to build a great city with a tower that would reach up into heaven, so that they would make a great name for themselves and not be scattered far from their great tower. Accordingly, they set to work in a wide plain to make bricks and to pile them higher and higher towards the sky.

But God stopped their proud and foolish plan. Suddenly their language was confused so that one part of the people could not understand what another part was saying. Then they stopped building and were scattered over the earth.

The city where they built was called Babel, which means *confusion*.

CHAPTER TWO

THE HISTORY OF THE PATRIARCHS

After the stories of the creation of the world and the early events of the human race, the Old Testament goes on to tell us of a number of very interesting men who stand out as the founders of the Hebrew nation, God's chosen people.

These men have been called *patriarchs,* which means fathers. All of them made their living by raising sheep and cattle. Their households were large. Being a shepherd people, they lived in tents and moved from place to place to find pasture for their flocks of sheep and herds of cattle.

In these stories we see how very frank the Bible is in its treatment of its heroes. The faults of these men are not covered up or excused. When they did wrong, the Bible tells it. Yet their names — Abraham, Isaac, Jacob, and Joseph — are better remembered than the names of many kings and generals. This is because these shepherd-patriarchs lived close to God, and when they sinned they repented and learned the ways of God. Theirs is the vivid story of real people struggling with the problems of life and being trained as a nation for their special calling as God's chosen people, among whom the knowledge of God was to be increased and preserved until the Saviour should come.

ABRAHAM

A man by the name of Abraham, a descendant of Shem, dwelt in Haran in Mesopotamia. To him the Lord said, "Get thee out of thy country, and from thy kindred, and from thy father's house, to a land that I will show thee. I will make of thee a great nation, and I will bless thee; and in thee shall all families of the earth be blessed." Abraham, therefore, took Sarah, his wife, and Lot, his brother's son, and all their possessions and went forth into the strip of country lying between the Mediterranean Sea and the Jordan Valley which we know as Palestine but which was then called the Land of Canaan. Abraham was at that time seventy-five years old. And the Lord appeared to Abraham and said, "Unto thy descendants will I give this land." And Abraham built an altar and worshipped God.

COPR. BY PROVIDENCE LITHOGRAPH CO.

Abraham was very rich in cattle, in silver, and in gold. Lot also had flocks and herds, and there was always strife between their herdsmen over the pastures. Then Abraham suggested to Lot that he should choose one part of the country and take that for his own, and Abraham would take the rest. "If you will take the land to the left," he said, "I will go to the right; or if you go to the right, I will go to the left."

This was very generous of Abraham, and Lot lost no time in taking selfish advantage of his uncle's love of peace. He looked to the east, where all the land was pleasant and well watered and said that he would go in that direction, toward the cities of Sodom and Gomorrah.

And the Lord said to Abraham, after Lot was separated from him, "All the land which thou seest, to thee will I give it, and to thy descendants for ever."

Not long after this there came into Lot's country strange kings, who raided the cities, took Lot captive, and carried off with them many of his possessions. As soon as Abraham heard this bad news, he gathered together three hundred of his servants, and set out in pursuit of the enemy. Soon he had rescued Lot, recovered his possessions, and brought him back to his home.

Abraham was troubled because he was childless, and said, "Lord, what wilt thou give me?" One night the Lord came to him and said, "Look now toward heaven and count the stars, if thou be able to number them! So shall thy seed be multiplied upon the earth." Abraham believed the Lord, and he counted it to him for righteousness.

When Abraham was ninety-nine years old, the Lord again appeared to him and confirmed his former promise, adding that he would make a covenant with him. In return, God required Abraham to serve him faithfully. God promised Abraham a son, whose name should be called Isaac.

After this the Lord appeared to Abraham in the plain of Mamre, which is in Hebron, as he sat in the tent door in the heat of the day. And he lifted up his eyes and looked, and lo, three men stood by him; and he ran to meet them, bowed himself toward the ground, and said, "My Lord, if I have found favor in thy sight, pass not away from thy servant!" The Lord said, "When I return unto thee a year hence, Sarah thy wife shall have a son." Sarah heard this and laughed within herself, for both she and Abraham were far advanced in age. But the Lord said, "Wherefore did Sarah laugh? Is anything too hard for the Lord?" And Sarah counted him faithful who had promised (Heb. 11:11).

SODOM AND GOMORRAH

In Sodom and Gomorrah the life of the people was wicked. But Lot had moved to that city, and whether or not he liked the place, it seemed that his wife and daughters did.

And the Lord said, "The cry of Sodom and Gomorrah is great, and their sin is very grievous." Because of their sin it was in the Lord's mind to destroy them.

But Abraham drew near to the Lord and said, "Perhaps there are fifty righteous in the city; be it far from thee to slay the righteous with the wicked!" And the Lord said, "If I find in Sodom fifty righteous within the city, then I will spare all the place for their sakes." But Abraham said, "Behold now, I have taken upon me to speak unto the Lord, which am dust and ashes, and have prayed the Lord to spare the city, if there should be found forty-five, or forty, or thirty, or twenty righteous." Finally Abraham said, "Let not the Lord be angry, and I will speak yet but this once! Perhaps ten shall be found there." The Lord said, "I will not destroy it for the sake of ten." And the Lord went his way, as soon as he had left speaking with Abraham; and Abraham returned to his place.

In the evening two angels came to Sodom. When Lot saw them he rose up to meet them, bowed down, and asked them to enter into his house and stay there all night. And they went into Lot's house.

"Whatever you have in the city, bring all out of this place, for we will destroy it," said the angels. Then Lot went out and told it to his sons-in-law, who were to marry his daughters; but they were no better than the rest of the people in the town, and they laughed at him.

And the angels laid hold upon Lot's hand and upon the hand of his wife and their two daughters and brought them out of the city, and said, "Escape for your life; do not look behind, and do not stop in the plain; escape to the mountain."

Then the Lord rained upon Sodom and Gomorrah brimstone and fire out of heaven, and he overthrew those cities and all the plain and all the inhabitants of the cities. But Lot's wife looked back and she became a pillar of salt.

ABRAHAM'S OBEDIENCE AND FAITH

As had been promised, a son was born to Abraham and Sarah in their old age. They called him Isaac and loved him dearly. Some years after this, God commanded Abraham to take his beloved son and to go up to Mount Moriah and there to sacrifice him as a burnt offering.

And Abraham rose up early in the morning, and saddled his ass, and took two of his young men with him, and Isaac his son, and wood for the burnt offering, and went to the place of which God had told him. On the third day Abraham saw the place afar off, and said to his young men, "Wait! I and the lad will go yonder and worship, and come again to you." Abraham took the wood of the burnt offering and laid it upon Isaac his son, and he took the fire in his hand, and a knife; and they went both of them together. And Isaac said, "Behold the fire and the wood; but where is the lamb for a burnt offering?" Abraham said, "My son, God will provide a lamb for a burnt offering." When they came to the place of which God had told him, Abraham built an altar, and laid the wood in order, and bound Isaac his son, and laid him on the altar upon the wood. And Abraham stretched forth his hand, and took the knife to sacrifice his son.

And the angel of the Lord called to him out of heaven, and said, "Abraham! Abraham! Lay not thy hand upon the lad, for now I know that thou fearest God, seeing thou hast not withheld thine only son from me." And Abraham lifted up his eyes and saw behind him a ram, caught in a thicket by his horns, and he took the ram, and offered him up for a burnt offering instead of his son.

And the Lord called to Abraham out of heaven the second time, and said, "Because thou hast done this thing, and hast not withheld thine only son, I will bless thee, and will multiply thy seed as the stars of heaven, and as the sand upon the seashore; and in thy seed shall all the nations of the earth be blessed, because thou hast obeyed my voice."

ISAAC MARRIES REBEKAH

When Isaac had grown to manhood, his father was anxious to choose for him a wife who feared God. So he called his oldest servant, and sent him into Mesopotamia in order that he might find a wife for Isaac among his own friends and kinsfolk.

And the servant took ten camels and departed, and came to Haran in Mesopotamia. And he made his camels to kneel down outside the city by a well of water. And he prayed, saying, "O Lord God of my master Abraham, send me good speed this day, and show kindness to my master Abraham! Let it come to pass that the damsel, coming to draw water, to whom I shall say: Let down thy pitcher, I pray thee, that I may drink; and she shall say: Drink, and I will give thy camels drink also; let the same be she that thou hast appointed for thy servant Isaac!"

Before he had finished speaking, Rebekah, the daughter of Bethuel, came out with her pitcher upon her shoulder. She went down to the well and filled her pitcher, and came up. And the servant ran to meet her, and said, "Let me, I pray thee, drink a little water of your pitcher." She said, "Drink, my lord! I will draw water for your camels also." When the camels had finished drinking, the man gave her a golden earring and two golden bracelets, and said, "Whose daughter are you?" She said, "I am the daughter of Bethuel." And the servant worshipped the Lord, and said, "Blessed be the Lord God, who has led me to the house of my master's kinsfolk." And Rebekah ran, and told her father whose name was Bethuel, and the rest of his family of this visitor from afar.

Rebekah had a brother by the name of Laban, who ran to meet the man. He brought him into the house and set food before him to eat. But he would not eat until he had told his errand. When he had done so, Laban and

Bethuel answered, "God has directed all these events. Rebekah shall go with you." Then he ate and drank, and stayed all night. The following morning, after Rebekah also had given her consent, he took her with him and departed for the home of his master. And she became Isaac's wife and he loved her. Abraham lived yet for some time, and died one hundred and seventy-five years old, and was buried in Mamre.

ESAU AND JACOB

Isaac and Rebekah had two sons, Esau and Jacob. Esau, the first-born, was red and hairy, and rough in his manners; Jacob, the younger, was smooth-skinned and of a gentle disposition. Esau became a hunter, a man of the field, while Jacob became a shepherd, living in tents. Isaac loved Esau and ate with delight the game which he had successfully hunted; but Rebekah loved rather the smooth and gentle Jacob.

One day Jacob had prepared a dish of pottage. Esau, who was returning from the field tired and hungry, asked for it. But Jacob refused unless Esau would give him his birthright for it. So Esau, thinking lightly of the matter, sold his birthright to Jacob, who was younger.

When Isaac had grown old and his eyes were dim, he called Esau and said to him, "Behold, now I am old, and I know not the day of my death. Go out to the field and take me some venison, and make me savoury meat, such as I love, that my soul may bless you before I die." And Esau went.

But Rebekah overheard these words. As soon as Esau had gone out, she called Jacob and had him bring quickly two young goats, so that she might prepare savoury meat for his father. Then she put Esau's clothes on Jacob and persuaded him to go in to his father with the meat, pretending to be Esau, so that he might receive the blessing intended for his brother. Jacob obeyed his mother, went in to his father, and said, "I am Esau, your first-born. Arise, sit and eat of my venison, that your soul may bless me!" At first Isaac was doubtful, but calling Jacob to him and touching him, he said, "The voice is the voice of Jacob, but the hands are the hands of Esau." So Isaac ate the savoury meat, and blessed Jacob.

But Jacob had scarcely gone out when Esau came in from his hunting. He also made savoury meat, and brought it to his father, and said, "Let my father arise, and eat of his son's venison, that he may bless me." And Isaac trembled and said, "Your brother came with deceitfulness, and took away your blessing."

Now Esau hated Jacob because of the blessing, and said in his heart, "I will slay my brother." When these words were told to Rebekah, she said to Jacob, "Arise, flee to Laban my brother, to Haran, and remain with him until your brother's fury shall turn away!" And Isaac also called his son Jacob, blessed him again, and said, "Do not take a wife of the daughters of Canaan, but go to Mesopotamia and take a wife from the daughters of Laban, your mother's brother! And God Almighty bless you, and give you the blessing of Abraham, to you, and to your descendants with you!"

JACOB'S FLIGHT

Jacob obeyed his father and his mother, and went to Mesopotamia. And he came to a certain place, and stayed there all night, because the sun had set. He took one of the stones of that place for a pillow, and lay down to sleep. And he dreamed that a ladder stood upon the earth, and the top of it reached to heaven; and the angels of God ascended and descended on it. And the Lord stood above it, and said, "I am the Lord God of Abraham and of Isaac. The land whereon thou liest, to thee will I give it, and to thy seed; and in thee and in thy seed shall all the families of the earth be blessed. I am with thee, and will keep thee whither thou goest, and will bring thee again into this land."

When Jacob awaked out of his sleep, he said, "Surely the Lord is in this place. This is none other than the house of God, and this is the gate of heaven." And he rose up, took the stone that he had used for his pillow, and setting it up for a sacred pillar, he poured oil upon it and called the place Beth-El (House of God). And he vowed that, if he should ever return, he would in that place build an altar to God and give to him a tenth of all his possessions.

Then Jacob continued his journey until he reached Mesopotamia. And he came to a well in the field. Soon Rachel, the daughter of Laban, his mother's brother, came there to water her father's sheep. When she was told that he was Isaac's and Rebekah's son, she ran and told her father. When Laban heard the news of Jacob, his sister's son, he ran to meet him, and brought him to his house.

JACOB WITH LABAN

When Jacob had been with Laban a month, Laban said, "Tell me, what shall your wages be?" Jacob answered, "I will serve you seven years for Rachel, your younger daughter." And the seven years seemed to him but a few days, for the love he had to her. But Laban deceived Jacob, and gave him Leah, his elder daughter, for a wife instead of Rachel. For Rachel Jacob had to serve seven years longer. After this Jacob served Laban six more years; and God blessed Jacob, so that he became very rich.

But Laban and his sons were jealous of Jacob on account of his wealth. And the Lord said to Jacob, "Return to the land of thy fathers, and to thy kindred! I will be with thee." Then Jacob rose up, took his family and all his possessions and returned again to the land of Canaan.

JACOB'S RETURN HOME

When Jacob arrived at the banks of the Jordan, he began to be afraid of meeting Esau. He then sent messengers laden with gifts to make peace with him; but without giving answer, Esau came to meet his brother, accompanied by four hundred men.

Then Jacob prayed to God, begging for help. "I am not worthy of the least of all the mercies, and of all the truth, which thou hast showed unto thy servant," he said. "Deliver me, I pray thee, from the hand of my brother."

During the night an angel appeared to him and wrestled with him until daybreak. And when he saw that he could not prevail against Jacob, he touched the hollow of his thigh; and the hollow of Jacob's thigh was out of joint. And he said, "Let me go!" But Jacob said, "I will not let thee go, except thou bless me." He said, "Thy name shall no more be called Jacob, but Israel; for as a prince hast thou fought with God and men, and hast prevailed." And he blessed him there. And Jacob said, "I have seen God face to face, and my life is saved!"

In the morning Jacob (now called Israel) saw Esau coming toward him with four hundred men. Having divided his family and his servants and his flocks into two companies, he went to meet his brother, bowing himself to the ground seven times before him. Then Esau ran to meet him, embraced him, and kissed him; and the brothers wept for joy. Jacob's children, also advancing, bowed themselves before Esau.

Thereupon Jacob urged his brother to receive the presents which he had sent, and the two brothers parted in peace.

Continuing his journey, Jacob came to Beth-El, where he built an altar, and God blessed him, saying, "I am God Almighty. Nations and kings shall be descended from thee, and the land which I gave to Abraham and Isaac, to thee will I give it, and to thy descendants after thee."

Finally Jacob and his family came to his father Isaac in Mamre. This brought much joy to the heart of the aged father, and he gave thanks to God that his son had returned. Isaac died at the advanced age of one hundred and eighty years, and was buried by his sons Esau and Jacob.

JOSEPH AND HIS BROTHERS

Jacob had twelve sons:

(1) Reuben	(5) Dan	(9) Issachar
(2) Simeon	(6) Naphtali	(10) Zebulun
(3) Levi	(7) Gad	(11) Joseph and
(4) Judah	(8) Asher	(12) Benjamin

Of all these sons, Joseph was the best, and his father loved him most. As a token of this love, Jacob gave Joseph a beautiful coat of many colors, such as a chief wore. This filled the brothers with anger and envy. One day, while the brothers were tending the flocks, they did something that would displease Jacob, and when Joseph told his father, they grew even more bitter toward him and could not speak a kind word to him.

Moreover, Joseph told his brothers of a dream he had had. They were all binding sheaves in the field, when suddenly his sheaf rose up, and theirs, standing round about, bowed down to his. When they heard this, they hated him all the more. Another time Joseph dreamed that the sun, the moon, and eleven stars seemed to bow to him. Even his father was displeased, and asked, "Shall your mother and I and your brothers all bow down to the earth for you?"

The Coat of Many Colors

37

Some time after this Jacob sent Joseph to see how his brothers were getting along tending the flocks at Shechem. When they saw him coming they said, "Look, here comes the dreamer! Let us kill him and put him in a pit." When Reuben heard it, he persuaded them not to take his life, but to let him down into the empty cistern that was nearby. This he did hoping that he might set him free and bring him to his father again.

So when Joseph reached his brothers, they stripped him of his coat of many colors and cast him into the empty cistern. Then they sat down to eat their food.

Looking up, they saw a caravan of Ishmaelite merchants on their way to Egypt, carrying spices and other valuable things on their camels. "Come," said Judah, "let us sell him to the Ishmaelites." So the brothers drew Joseph out of the pit and sold him for twenty pieces of silver. And the Ishmaelites took Joseph with them to Egypt, though he was only seventeen years old.

Then the brothers killed a young goat, dipped the coat of many colors in his blood, brought it to Jacob, and told him they had found it. Jacob recognized the coat at once, and concluded that a wild beast had devoured his son. And Jacob mourned many days, refusing to be comforted. "I will go down into the grave mourning," he said.

JOSEPH IN EGYPT

When the Ishmaelites came to Egypt, they sold Joseph to Potiphar, a high officer in the army of Pharaoh, the king. God was with Joseph, so that he prospered in whatever he did. Soon Potiphar placed him in charge of his house and all that he had, and the Lord blessed the Egyptian's house for Joseph's sake.

Then Potiphar's wife tried to lead Joseph into a shameful sin, but he refused, saying, "How can I do this great wickedness and sin against God?" Then she decided to take revenge on the young man by falsely accusing him of wrong. Potiphar believed her lie, and became so angry that he had Joseph put in prison.

But the Lord was with Joseph so that he found favor with the keeper of the prison. Now it happened that the king's butler and baker were put in the same prison. One morning Joseph found both of them very sad because of dreams that they had during the night. When they told Joseph their dreams, he interpreted them, explaining that the butler's dream meant that he would be restored to his place but the baker's dream meant that he was to be hanged. Three days later the dreams came true.

Before the butler was released, Joseph asked him to remember him when he had returned to his work. But he soon forgot about Joseph.

Two years after this Pharaoh had a strange dream. He seemed to stand on the bank of the Nile, while seven fat cows came up and fed in the meadow; then seven other cows came up, thin and ugly, and ate up the fat cows. In another dream he saw seven ears of grain growing on a single stalk, full and plump, and after them there sprouted seven other ears, thin, empty, and withered by the east wind. And the thin ears swallowed up the full ears.

In the morning the king sent for all the wise-men of Egypt, but none of them could interpret his dreams. Then the butler remembered Joseph and told Pharaoh of the young man in prison. So Pharaoh sent for Joseph. When the king related his dreams, Joseph said to the king: "God has shown Pharaoh what he is about to do. The seven good cows and the seven good ears are seven years of plenty, but the seven thin cows and the seven empty ears are seven years of famine. Behold, there shall come seven years of great plenty throughout all the land of Egypt, and after them there shall be seven years of famine. Now, therefore, let Pharaoh choose a good man to gather all the food of the good years and lay up grain for the seven years of famine, so that the land shall not perish because of the famine."

Pharaoh was pleased with this advice and, seeing that Joseph was wise and prudent, he chose him to be overseer over all Egypt. Then he took the signet ring from his own

"Joseph was chosen overseer over all Egypt"

39

finger and put it on Joseph's; he dressed him in white silken robes, put a gold chain round his neck, and had him ride in the second of his chariots, with heralds going before to shout, "Let all the people bow down!" So Joseph was put in charge of all Egypt.

At this time Joseph was thirty years old. And he stored up all the food of the good years. When the lean years came, he opened up the storehouses and sold food to all who came.

JOSEPH'S BROTHERS GO TO EGYPT

People from many countries came to Egypt to buy grain, for the famine was great in all lands. There was also famine in the land of Canaan. So when Jacob heard that there was grain in Egypt, he sent his sons there to buy; but Benjamin, his youngest son, he kept at home.

When the brothers came to Egypt, they bowed down before Joseph; and he knew them, though they did not know him, and he remembered his dream. He acted like a stranger to them, and accused them of being spies, but they answered that they were innocent, and had only come to buy food. "We are honest men, and not spies," they said. "Thy servants are twelve brothers; the youngest is at home with our father, and the other is dead." But Joseph, in order to test them further, had them put into prison.

On the third day Joseph said to them, "If you are honest men, let one of you brothers remain in prison, and then the rest of you may go and take with you grain for your families; but you must bring me your youngest brother."

When the brothers saw how severely they were treated, they began to speak among themselves. Not thinking that Joseph heard them, they blamed themselves for having treated their brother so shamefully. "When he pleaded with us in his distress, we paid no attention," they said, "and now we are being justly punished." When Joseph heard this, he turned away and wept.

Coming back to them, Joseph took Simeon and had him imprisoned. Then he ordered that their sacks be filled with grain and their money put secretly in each man's sack. Provisions were also given for their journey. When they returned home, they told their father all that had happened. And when they emptied their sacks, each found his money with the grain. And fear came upon both them and their father.

"I am Joseph, your brother"

41

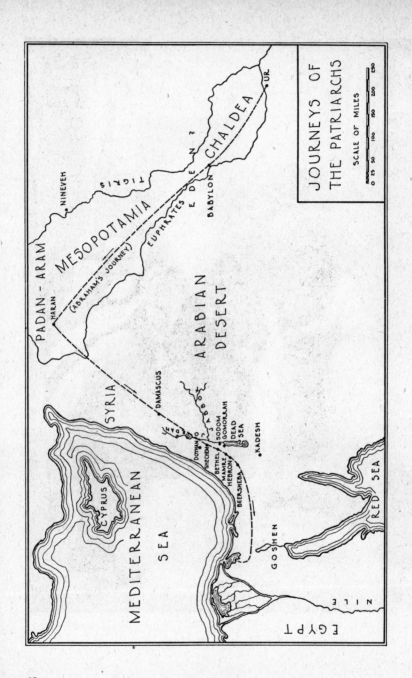

JOURNEYS OF
THE PATRIARCHS

SCALE OF MILES

0 25 50 100 150 200 250

NINEVEH

MESOPOTAMIA

PADAN - ARAM

HARAN

(ABRAHAM'S JOURNEY)

EUPHRATES

TIGRIS

E D E N ?

CHALDEA

BABYLON

UR

ARABIAN DESERT

DAMASCUS

SYRIA

JORDAN

JABBOK

DOTHAN

SHECHEM

BETHEL

MAMRE

HEBRON

BEERSHEBA

SODOM

GOMORRAH

DEAD SEA

KADESH

CYPRUS

MEDITERRANEAN SEA

GOSHEN

RED SEA

NILE

EGYPT

42

THE SECOND JOURNEY TO EGYPT

When their food was all gone, Jacob sent his sons back to Egypt to buy more grain. But Jacob objected to having Benjamin go with them. Then Judah said it would be useless to go unless Benjamin was with them. So Jacob answered, "Take of the best things in the land and carry the man a present; and the money that was brought again in your sacks bring also with you. But God Almighty give you mercy before the man, that he may send away your other brother and Benjamin!"

When they arrived in Egypt, Joseph received them kindly and asked, "Is your father well? Is he yet alive?" And when he saw Benjamin, Joseph's heart was so touched that he hurried to his room and wept. Then when he had washed his face, he went out again.

Joseph commanded his steward to make a feast for the brothers. Seeing what was done, they became frightened and began to think it was because of the money they had found in their sacks. But the steward told them not to be afraid, and went to bring Simeon to join them.

At the feast they were placed according to the order of their age, and Benjamin's share of good food was five times as much as that of any of the others.

When the feast was ended, Joseph bade his steward fill the sacks with grain, put each man's money back into his sack, and include his own silver cup in the sack of the youngest.

The next morning they set out for home. Before they had gone very far, Joseph's steward overtook them and accused them of having stolen his master's silver cup. The brothers answered that if any one of them could be found having the cup, he should die. Hurriedly the sacks were opened, and the cup was found in Benjamin's. Filled with fear, they were brought back to Joseph.

Judah begged Joseph not to harm Benjamin, and offered to die in his place. "If we go back to our father," he said, "and the lad is not with us, we shall bring down the gray hairs of our father with sorrow to the grave. Let me take his place, so that the lad may go back with his brothers."

Then Joseph wept aloud and said, "I am Joseph your brother." But his brothers were so frightened that they could not answer him. Then he said, "Do not think that I am angry; God sent me here for your welfare." And he kissed his brothers and they talked with him.

Five years of the famine remained, so Joseph asked that his father and all his brothers move to Egypt. Both Joseph and Pharaoh sent many presents to Jacob. As the brothers took leave of Joseph, he said, "See that you do not quarrel on the way."

ISRAEL IN EGYPT

When the brothers came home, they told their father that Joseph was alive and was ruler of all Egypt. At first Israel did not believe them, but when he saw the gifts he said, "It is enough; my son Joseph is alive. I will go and see him, before I die."

Then Israel gathered together all his possessions and journeyed with his family to Egypt. And when he came to Beer-sheba, God said to him, "Fear not to go down into Egypt, for I will make of thee a great nation. I will go down with thee into Egypt."

Judah went on before to tell Joseph that his father was coming. Joseph hastened to meet him. When he saw him, he fell on his neck and wept for joy.

As Pharaoh had commanded, Joseph placed his father and brothers in the land of Goshen, in the best part of Egypt. And Joseph provided food for them and all their households during the famine.

Israel lived in the land of Egypt for seventeen years and died there. As he himself had planned, his sons buried him in the cave before Mamre in the land of Canaan, with Abraham and Isaac.

CHAPTER THREE

THE MAKING OF A NATION

The first book of the Bible, the book of Genesis, closes with the death of Joseph. Next comes the book of Exodus. As the ancient accounts in Genesis have told of Abraham and the other patriarchs in Canaan and finally in Egypt, so Exodus and other history books that follow relate how the children of Israel were led from Egypt back to Canaan and formed into a nation.

Following the death of Joseph and the Pharaoh who had raised him to a high position, conditions changed for the descendants of Israel. They were no longer popular. The Egyptians thought that they were crowding them out of their best land. They did not like their ways, and began to fear and hate them. Finally a new Pharaoh came to the throne who determined to make slaves of the Israelites. He compelled them to work on great building projects, making brick and erecting perhaps such monuments as the pyramids or great palace buildings. This period lasted several hundred years.

Although Pharaoh put hard taskmasters over the Israelites and made their lives bitter, these people continued to grow in numbers. This made the king fearful, so he issued an order that all their boy children, as soon as they were born, should be drowned in the Nile.

One little boy, however, escaped this cruel attempt, and was brought up in the king's own court as the adopted son of the king's daughter. His name was Moses, and under the Providence of God he became the leader of his people. Around him and his brother Aaron the people rallied to be led from bondage in Egypt to Canaan, the Promised Land. Forever afterward the Jews looked back to this great man not only as the one who delivered their ancestors from slavery in Egypt, but also as the servant through whom God made known the Law by which their lives were to be ordered.

To Joshua fell the honor of leading Israel into the Promised Land. Because of their little faith and much disobedience the people were forced to wander forty years in the wilderness and the desert. Most of them died without ever seeing the Promised Land, but under the leadership of Joshua their children settled in this land which had been promised to Abraham and his descendants. After years of warfare the twelve tribes of the twelve sons of Jacob conquered or drove out the inhabitants and occupied most of the land. The account includes many stories of hard struggle and great heroism. During these years the people were ruled by the Judges, who succeeded Joshua. These men were both military and political leaders, directing the wars and enforcing the laws. The last of the Judges was Samuel, who anointed the first of Israel's kings, since the people had determined to be ruled by a king.

MOSES

Goshen was a fertile land well suited for pasture. It was specially adapted to the needs of the children of Israel, who were a shepherd people. They increased and grew strong in numbers. But when Joseph and all who lived at this time were dead, there arose a new king over Egypt, who was not friendly to these descendants of Israel. He was afraid that they would join his enemies. He therefore compelled the children of Israel to build new cities, and he and the Egyptians afflicted them with heavy burdens. But the more they were afflicted, the more they multiplied and grew. Then Pharaoh commanded his people to cast all Hebrew boys into the river Nile.

Among the Israelites was a family to whom a boy was born; they already had one son whose name was Aaron and a daughter whose name was Miriam. For three months the mother managed to hide the baby. Then, knowing

Underwood and Underwood Photo

Scene from the Nile Valley

Pyramids in Egypt

that the Egyptians might discover him and kill him, she wove a little basket of bulrushes and made it water-tight with pitch, so that it floated like a boat. In it she placed the baby and left it among the reeds by the edge of the river. A distance away she put Miriam to watch and see what would happen.

Down to this very spot came the daughter of Pharaoh with her maidens to bathe in the river. When she saw the little basket floating among the reeds, she sent one of her maids to get it. When she opened the top of the basket, she saw the baby, and the baby cried.

She felt sorry for the little boy and said, "This is one of the Hebrew's children." Just then Miriam came up to her and asked whether she would not like her to go and find a nurse among the Hebrew women to take care of the child. Pharaoh's daughter told her to go, so Miriam went and called the baby's own mother. When the mother came, the princess said, "Take this child and nurse it for me, and I will give you wages." So the mother took the child and nursed it. The boy grew and she took him to the princess, and he became her son. Moses was his name.

Moses grew up as a prince in the household of Pharaoh. Though he had many privileges, he could not forget the suffering of his own people. One day as he went about he saw an Egyptian taskmaster striking a Hebrew with his whip. In anger Moses struck the Egyptian so hard that he killed him. Then he hid his body in the sand.

Soon the report came to Pharaoh, and when he heard it, he said that Moses

47

should be put to death. But Moses escaped as quickly as he could, fleeing to the land of Midian, which is Arabia. Here he made his home with a priest by the name of Jethro and married one of the priest's daughters. To earn a living, he tended the flocks of his father-in-law.

Meanwhile the woes of the Hebrew people in Egypt were growing worse. Pharaoh had redoubled his oppression and the people were crying out to God for deliverance.

Nor had Moses forgotten his own people. Then, one day, as he had driven his flock to the slopes of Mount Horeb (Sinai), the angel of the Lord appeared to him in a flame of fire out of a bush, but the bush was not consumed. The voice of God called to him out of the bush and bade him return to Egypt, to lead his people out of slavery. At first Moses objected, saying that he was slow of speech, but God promised to be with him, and told him that Aaron, his brother, was to go with him to be spokesman.

So Moses returned to Egypt, and on the way Aaron met him. In Egypt they sent word calling all the chief men together. Aaron explained that God had promised them their freedom, and Moses did signs before them. And the people believed, and bowed their heads and worshipped God.

THE ISRAELITES SET FREE

Afterward Moses and Aaron appeared before Pharaoh and said, "Thus saith the Lord God of Israel: Let my people go." But Pharaoh answered in anger, "Who is this God of yours, that I should obey him? I do not know him and I will not let these Israelites go." And the same day Pharaoh commanded the taskmasters to give the people even more work than before.

Again Moses and Aaron went to Pharaoh, but he still refused to let the people go. Then God sent ten plagues upon Pharaoh and his people. The water of the Nile was turned into blood, the fish in the river died, and the water became so foul that the people could not drink it. After seven days frogs came up and covered the whole land. Then came lice that tormented both man and beast.

But Pharaoh hardened his heart against the Lord, and would not let the people go.

In quick succession followed swarms of flies, disease among the cattle, and boils upon both man and beast. For the seventh plague God sent hail and lightning. After this came a plague of locusts to eat up what the hail had spared, and, at last, a thick darkness covered all the land of Egypt.

Several times Pharaoh promised to let the people go, but when he saw that a plague was ending, he would harden his heart and forbid the Israelites to leave. Finally the Lord struck him with a plague more terrible than the rest.

Before God sent the final plague he commanded the Israelites to make ready for it. Each family was told to prepare a lamb without spot or blemish and offer it for a sacrifice. They were required to sprinkle their door-posts with its blood, and to roast the lamb at the fire. Then, as they ate the lamb hurriedly with unleavened bread and bitter herbs, they were to stand with their sandals on and dressed for a journey. "For the angel of God will pass through Egypt this night," said Moses, "and he will take the life of the first-born in every family of the Egyptians; but when the angel sees the sign of the blood upon any house, he shall pass that house by."

About the middle of the night the plague fell upon Egypt, and in every family there was mourning because of the death of the first-born. Only the Israelites were spared, for when the angel of the Lord saw the sign of blood upon the door-posts, he passed the house by.

Then Pharaoh, filled with dismay, commanded Moses and Aaron to leave and take the Israelites with them. So the Israelites rose up and followed their leader northward out of Egypt.

This is how the Jewish people came to celebrate every year, down through the centuries, the feast of the Passover, to remind them how God had passed them by, pardoned their sins, and delivered them from slavery.

Escape from Egypt

THE PASSAGE THROUGH THE RED SEA

The Lord led the way for the Israelites, going before them by day in a pillar of cloud, and by night in a pillar of fire, so that they might travel both by day and by night. And they journeyed toward the Red Sea.

Soon Pharaoh regretted that he had let the Israelites go, so he gathered together his horsemen and chariots and set out in pursuit. When the Israelites saw the Egyptians behind them and the Red Sea before them, they were overcome with fear and began to blame Moses. But Moses answered, "Fear not. Stand still, and you shall see how God will save you."

Then God commanded Moses, "Lift up thy rod and stretch it over the water, and speak to the people that they go forward."

And the Lord caused the sea to go back by a strong wind from the east so that the waters were divided and there was passage across the bottom of the sea. Then the children of Israel crossed over this dry ground.

The Egyptians followed in pursuit. When the children of Israel had reached the other shore, God commanded Moses to stretch out his hand again over the sea. In a short time the wind went down, the waters returned, and the army of Pharaoh were drowned in the sea. Then Moses and the Israelites sang a song of praise and thanksgiving to the Lord for saving them from destruction at the hands of Pharaoh.

THE JOURNEY TO SINAI

From the Red Sea the children of Israel journeyed through desert country toward Mount Sinai. But when they could not find food, they began to complain against Moses and Aaron and to say that they wished that they were back in Egypt, where they had all the food they wanted.

But God promised them food. In the evening there came near the camp a great number of quail, which were easily caught. In the morning the ground was covered with small white things that looked like hoar-frost, but tasted like wafers made with honey. Moses told the people it was manna, the bread which the Lord had sent from heaven; and they were allowed to gather every day as much of it as was needed for the day, but on the sixth day of each week they were to gather enough for two days, for on the Sabbath there was none to be gathered.

At another time the people had no water to drink. Then they complained to Moses, and said, "Give us water!" Moses said to them, "Why do you tempt the Lord?" And he cried to the Lord, saying, "What shall I do unto these people? They are almost ready to stone me." The Lord said to him, "Take thy rod, wherewith thou smotest the river, and go! Behold, I will stand before thee there upon the rock in Horeb; and thou shalt smite the rock, and there shall come water out of it." Moses did as God commanded him, and the children of Israel drank of the water.

Then the Amalekites came and fought with the Israelites. And Moses sent Joshua to fight them while he himself went up to the top of a hill with the rod of God in his hand. And when Moses held up his hand, Israel prevailed; but when he let down his hand, Amalek prevailed. And Aaron and Hur helped Moses hold up his hands; and thus Israel conquered.

THE GIVING OF THE LAW

In the third month after the departure from Egypt the children of Israel came to Sinai. And the Lord said to Moses, "Thus shalt thou say to Israel: If ye will obey my voice and keep my covenant, then ye shall be my very own above all the peoples, and ye shall be unto me a kingdom of priests and a holy nation." Moses laid before the people all these words, and the people answered, "All that the Lord hath spoken we will do." And the Lord said to Moses, "Sanctify the people today and tomorrow, and let them wash their clothes, for on the third day the Lord will come down upon Mount Sinai in the sight of all the people."

On the third day there were thunders and lightnings, and a thick cloud upon the mountain, and the blast of a trumpet exceeding loud; and the people trembled. Then Moses brought the people out of the camp to meet with God; and they stood at the foot of the mountain. And the Lord descended upon the mountain, and spoke all these words:

"I am the Lord thy God, who brought thee out of the land of Egypt, out of the house of bondage."

"Thou shalt have no other gods before me. Thou shalt not make unto thee any graven image, or any likeness of any thing that is in heaven above, or that is in the earth beneath, or that is in the water under the earth. Thou shalt not bow down thyself to them, nor serve them. For I the Lord thy God am a jealous God, visiting the iniquity of the fathers upon the children, upon the third and upon the fourth generation of them that hate me; and showing loving kindness unto thousands of them that love me, and keep my commandments."

"Thou shalt not take the name of the Lord thy God in vain; for the Lord will not hold him guiltless, that taketh his name in vain.

"Remember the sabbath day, to keep it holy. Six days shalt thou labor, and do all thy work; but the seventh day is the sabbath of the Lord thy God; in it thou shalt not do any work, thou, nor thy son, nor thy daughter, thy manservant, nor thy maidservant, nor thy cattle, nor thy stranger that is within thy gates. For in six days the Lord made heaven and earth, the sea, and all that in them is, and rested the seventh day. Wherefore the Lord blessed the sabbath day, and hallowed it."

"Honor thy father and thy mother, that thy days may be long upon the land, which the Lord thy God giveth thee."

"Thou shalt not kill."

"Thou shalt not commit adultery."

"Thou shalt not steal."

"Thou shalt not bear false witness against thy neighbor."

"Thou shalt not covet thy neighbor's house."

"Thou shalt not covet thy neighbor's wife, nor his manservant, nor his maidservant, nor his ox, nor his ass, nor anything that is thy neighbor's."

And all the people saw the thunderings, and lightnings, and the noise of the trumpet; and they were afraid and fled, and said to Moses, "Speak thou with us, and we will listen; but let not God speak with us, lest we die."

At the command of the Lord, Moses went up into the midst of the cloud on the mountain and remained there forty days and forty nights. There the Lord gave him the Ten Commandments, written with the finger of God on two tables of stone. These commandments and other laws were given him to teach to the people.

THE IDOLATRY OF THE PEOPLE

When the people saw that Moses delayed coming down from the mountain, they gathered together and demanded that Aaron should make for

At Sinai

53

them gods like those of the Egyptians. Aaron obeyed the people, took their earrings and made a golden calf. And they said, "This is the god which brought us up out of the land of Egypt." Then they offered burnt offerings to the image; and the people sat down to eat and to drink, and rose up to play, after the manner of pagans.

When Moses came down from the mountain and saw the idolatry of the people, he became very angry, and throwing down the tablets on which the commandments were written, he broke them. And he took the calf which they had made, and burnt it with fire, and ground it to powder, and strewed it upon the water, and made the people drink of it.

Moses again returned to the mountain and prayed to the Lord for the people, saying, "They have sinned a great sin. Yet now, if thou wilt forgive their sin . . . and if not, blot me, I pray thee, out of thy book." And the Lord heard his prayer. And He commanded Moses to make two new tablets of stone like the first, and God again wrote on them the Ten Commandments.

HOW THE PEOPLE WERE TO WORSHIP GOD

Besides the Ten Commandments which God gave Moses, he also gave many rules pertaining to the public worship. With great care Moses established these as God commanded him.

The Lord said to Moses, "Speak to the children of Israel, that they make me a place of worship, that I may dwell among them. And the tabernacle and all the instruments thereof ye shall make after the pattern that I show thee." And every man gave willingly with his heart all that was required.

Underwood and Underwood Photo   *View of Mount Sinai*

The Encampment at Sinai

So Moses began by constructing a tent which was to be a sign of the presence of God among the people. The supports and poles were so framed that they could easily be taken apart. The length was about fifty feet, the width fifteen and the height fifteen. The supports were overlaid with gold, and the whole frame was covered with precious hangings.

The tent-church was divided into two rooms, separated by a veil. The outer room, which was the larger, was called the Sanctuary, or Holy Place, and the inner room, which was smaller, was called the Holy of Holies, or Most Holy Place.

Within the Most Holy Place was placed the Ark of the Covenant, a small box made of precious wood, overlaid with gold and surrmounted by two cherubim. In the Ark were placed the two tables of the Law.

Within the Holy Place were kept three objects set aside for the worship of God: the Table of Show-bread, on which were placed every sabbath day twelve loaves of bread; the Golden Candlestick which, with its seven lights, shone during the entire night; and the Altar of Incense, on which was burned the finest incense.

Surrounding the tabernacle was an inclosed court. Here was placed the Altar of Burnt-offering, upon which the offering was to be burned. Near the entrance to the Holy Place stood also the Laver, or great brass basin, at which the priests were to wash before they performed their service.

The sacrifices of the Old Testament included such offerings as heifers, sheep, goats, doves, and grain.

Every day the priests entered the Holy Place to burn incense before the Lord; but into the Most Holy Place only the high-priest could go. Once a year, on the Day of Atonement, he was to enter and bring a sin offering as an atonement for his own sins, and for the sins of the people.

The ministers of worship were to offer sacrifices, to pray for the people, and to pronounce the blessing of God upon them. There were these classes: (1) *The priests*, who were to offer sacrifice. This service was assigned to the sons of Aaron, of the tribe of Levi. (2) *The high-priest.* To this office Moses consecrated Aaron, anointing him and clothing him with special vestments. After Aaron, the oldest son of the family was to be the high-priest. (3) *The Levites*, who were of the tribe of Levi and were charged with lower offices within the Tabernacle, such as singing in the choir.

On the seventh day of each week the sabbath was to be observed, beginning at six o'clock the evening before. Strict laws forbade work and travel. In addition to the laws governing the sabbath, there were four important religious festivals each year:

a. *The Passover*, celebrated in remembrance of the deliverance from bondage in Egypt.

b. *Pentecost*, celebrated seven weeks after the Passover, in remembrance of the receiving of the Law on Mount Sinai. It was also a feast of thanksgiving after the harvest.

c. *Tabernacles*, in memory of the many years in the wilderness. During this feast the Israelites were required to live in tents or booths made from the branches of trees.

d. *The Day of Atonement*, when the high-priest offered sacrifice for his own sins and for the sins of the people.

THE WANDERING IN THE WILDERNESS

About a year later, the Israelites journeyed onward and came to the southern border of the land of Canaan. At the command of the Lord, Moses sent twelve spies, one from each tribe, to see the land and the people that lived there. After forty days they returned, bringing some of the fruit of the land, and said, "The land flows with milk and honey; but the people are stronger than we, and the cities are walled and very great. We are not able to go up against these people. We saw giants, and in their sight we were as grasshoppers."

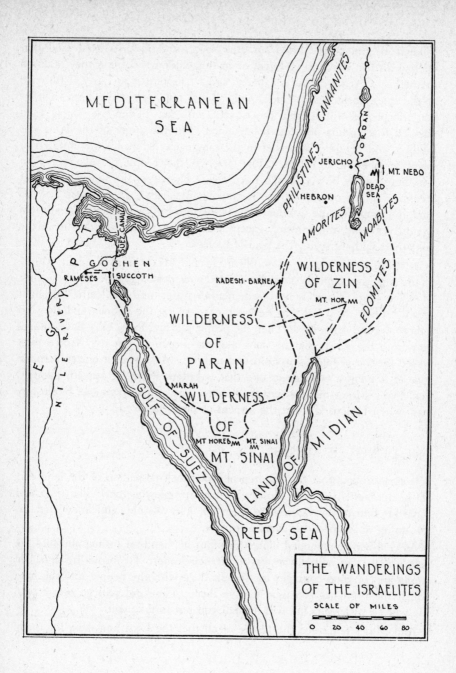

MEDITERRANEAN
SEA

PHILISTINES
CANAANITES
JERICHO
MT. NEBO
HEBRON
DEAD
SEA
AMORITES
MOABITES

SUEZ CANAL

GOSHEN
RAMESES
SUCCOTH

KADESH-BARNEA

WILDERNESS
OF ZIN

MT. HOR

EDOMITES

WILDERNESS
OF
PARAN

NILE RIVER

MARAH

WILDERNESS
OF
MT. SINAI

GULF OF SUEZ

MT HOREB
MT. SINAI

LAND OF MIDIAN

RED SEA

THE WANDERINGS
OF THE ISRAELITES

SCALE OF MILES

0   20   40   60   80

Then all the people lifted up their voice, and said, "Would God that we had died in the land of Egypt or in this wilderness!" And they said one to another, "Let us choose a captain, and let us return to Egypt!" But two of the spies, Joshua and Caleb, said, "Rebel not against the Lord, neither fear the people of the land; the Lord is with us." Then the people commanded that Joshua and Caleb be stoned. But the anger of the Lord was kindled, and his glory appeared in the tabernacle before all the children of Israel, and he said to Moses, "How long will this people provoke me? And how long will it be ere they believe me?" Thereupon he announced, that according to the number of the forty days in which they had searched the land, the people should wander in the wilderness forty years; and that all from twenty years old and upward, except Joshua and Caleb, should die in the wilderness without seeing the land of promise.

Later the people journeyed southward to compass the land of Edom. While on the way, the people became discouraged and spoke against God and against Moses, saying, "There is no bread, neither water, and we loathe this light bread." Then the Lord sent fiery serpents among the people, and they bit the people; and many died. Then the people said to Moses, "We have sinned; pray unto the Lord, that he may take the serpents from us!" And Moses prayed for the people. The Lord said to him, "Make thee a brazen serpent, and set it upon a pole; every one that is bitten, when he looketh upon it, shall live." Moses made a serpent of brass, and if a serpent had bitten any man, when he looked up at the serpent of brass, he lived.

THE DEATH OF MOSES

It came to pass that the children of Israel took possession of the land east of the Jordan. After this Moses called his people together. The time had come for him to say farewell to them all. He was old, and knew that his remaining days upon this earth were few.

As God had commanded him, Moses put his hand on Joshua and told the people that from now on he was to be their leader. To Joshua he said, "Be strong and of good courage: for you shall go with the people into the land which the Lord has promised to give them. The Lord will go before you. He will be with you. He will not fail you nor forsake you."

And Moses reminded the people of all that the Lord had done for them;

how he had freed them from Egypt and provided for them in the wilderness. And he commanded them to keep the commandments, to love the Lord, and to obey his voice.

After this Moses went up to Mount Nebo, to the top of Pisgah, across from Jericho. Here the Lord showed him the land of Canaan. And the Lord said, "This is the land I promised to Abraham, and Isaac, and Jacob, saying, I will give it unto thy seed."

And Moses died in the land of Moab, full of gratitude to God, at the age of a hundred and twenty years. All Israel mourned his death, and there was never a prophet like Moses.

THE ISRAELITES ENTER THE PROMISED LAND

After the death of Moses, the Lord said to Joshua, "Arise, go over this Jordan, thou and all this people, unto the land which I do give to them. As I was with Moses, so will I be with thee. Be strong and of good courage, for unto this people shalt thou divide the land for an inheritance."

Joshua commanded the people to go forward across the Jordan River. The priests took the Ark of the Covenant and marched before the people. And when the feet of the priests touched the brim of the water, the waters above ceased flowing, while the waters below ran down, leaving a dry passage for the people to cross over. And the priests that carried the Ark stood firm on dry ground in the midst of the Jordan, until all the people had passed over.

COPR. BY PROVIDENCE LITHOGRAPH CO.

"The priests took the Ark of the Covenant and marched before the people"

The people encamped near Jericho, where they celebrated the feast of the Passover. From now on the manna ceased, and the Israelites used the grain of the land for food.

At Jericho, a strongly walled city, the captain of the host of the Lord appeared to Joshua. At the command of the Lord the warriors went around the walls of the city each day for six succeeding days. On the seventh day the priests carried with them the Ark of the Covenant, while seven priests sounded the trumpets and the people shouted with a great cry. At the sound of the trumpets and the shout of the people, the walls fell to the ground, and the Israelites took the city.

In time, Joshua conquered all the land of Canaan, both hill country and lowlands. By casting lot, he divided the country among the twelve tribes of Israel. At last the land had rest from war. All that God had promised the Israelites came to pass.

When Joshua had grown old, he called together all the tribes of Israel. He reminded them of God's wonderful guidance and urged them to serve the Lord sincerely and faithfully. "But if it seem evil unto you to serve the Lord," said he, "choose this day whom ye will serve. But as for me and my house, we will serve the Lord." The people answered and said, "God forbid that we should forsake the Lord, to serve other gods! We also will serve the Lord, for he is God." So Joshua made a covenant with the people that day, and he took a great stone and set it up there for a token of the covenant.

And Joshua, the servant of the Lord, died, being one hundred and ten years old.

THE JUDGES

After the death of Joshua, the children of Israel served the Lord as long as the older people lived who had seen the great works of the Lord in the wilderness. But the younger generation soon forgot the Lord and forsook him for the worship of idols. To punish them for their wrong, the Lord delivered them into the hands of enemies.

In their distress the people cried to the Lord for help, and he sent upright men, called judges, chosen from among the people, to lead them to freedom and to rule over them in a simple but just way. Otherwise in those days every man did what was right in his own eyes. The whole period of the judges lasted about three hundred years. It was a time when people turned from God to worship idols, then were punished; after which they returned to God in repentance, only to slip back again into the old sins.

GIDEON

One of the greatest of the judges was Gideon. The children of Israel had done evil in the sight of the Lord, and He delivered them into the hands of the Midianites seven years. Then God called Gideon to destroy the altar of Baal that his father owned and to build an altar for the Lord instead. Gideon was also to set the Israelites free from the Midianites.

So Gideon gathered an army of thirty-two thousand men, but the Lord told him there were too many, saying that if they should succeed in defeating the Midianites, they would vaunt themselves against God instead of recognizing their need for his help. At last Gideon kept only three hundred men. To each man he gave a trumpet and also an empty pitcher, with a lamp within the pitcher. That night he led them to the camp of the enemy, and his men blew the trumpets, and broke the pitchers so that their lights suddenly began to show all about, and they cried, "The sword of the Lord and of Gideon!" Taken by surprise, the Midianites fled in confusion.

Thankful for Gideon's leadership, the people asked Gideon to become their ruler, and his son after him. But Gideon was too humble a man to make himself king. "The Lord shall rule over you," he said, and the country was in quietness the next forty years, as long as Gideon lived. After his death the children of Israel again turned to other gods.

SAMSON

Another of the judges was Samson. He was a Nazirite, that is, a person pledged to lead a very strict life, to drink no wine, and never to cut his hair. So great was Samson's strength that, on one occasion, by the mere power of his hands, he tore a furious lion to pieces. When he was judge over the Israelites they were being oppressed by the neighboring Philistines. Samson went to Gaza, where the people of the town laid wait for him all night, saying, "When day dawns, we will kill him." But at midnight Samson arose, took hold of the doors of the city and its two posts, lifted them up, posts and all, and carried them off to the top of a mountain.

Now Samson had fallen in love with a woman named Delilah. The leaders of the Philistines bribed her to find out for them how Samson could be so strong. She kept pressing him to tell her the secret, but he would not give the answer. Finally, however, he told her that if his hair should be cut, his strength would be gone. When he was asleep, she called the Philistines. They shaved off his hair, bound him, and put out his eyes.

Samson was kept a prisoner and compelled to grind grain. One day while the Philistines were feasting and making merry over a victory, Samson was brought out so they could make sport of him. Wearied, he leaned against the pillars that supported the building in which the Philistines had gathered. He prayed to God, begging that his old strength might return. His prayer was heard. With mighty power he tore loose the pillars so that they slipped off their pedestals and the whole building fell, killing both him and the great crowd of Philistines.

SAMUEL

Hannah and Elkanah had a son who was named Samuel. For a long time the devout mother had prayed for a son, and when he was born she dedicated him to the service of God. While he was still only a boy she took him to Shiloh, to the house of the Lord, so that he might be a helper to Eli, the high-priest and judge.

One night as Samuel slept in the tabernacle, God called him. He thought the voice was Eli's, and he ran to him to see what he wanted. But Eli had not called him, and he told him to listen again, for it must be the voice of

God. The Lord then said to Samuel that he would punish Eli and his family because of the iniquity of his sons. For the sons of Eli were wicked men, and when their father urged them to do what was right, they would not listen.

Soon the punishment came. In a battle with the Philistines two sons of Eli took with them the ark of the Lord, thinking that in some magical way it would help them in battle. But the Philistines were victorious; they killed thousands of Israelites, among them the sons of Eli, and took the ark. When Eli heard this, he was so terrified that he fell from his seat and died.

Later, the Philistines sent back the ark, for it brought them much trouble at the hand of God, and they were relieved to be rid of it.

Samuel now became judge of the Israelites, and he spoke to them saying that if they would return to the Lord with all their hearts and put away their idols, the Lord would deliver them out of the hand of the Philistines. The Israelites promised to do this. Led by Samuel they were victorious over the Philistines. Samuel judged his people justly and was respected by all; but his sons, who were judges after him, were not as good as their father.

RUTH

During the time of the judges there arose a famine in the land, and a certain man from Bethlehem went, with his wife and two sons, into the country of the heathen Moabites. His sons married women of Moab. Later both the man and his two sons died.

Then the mother, whose name was Naomi, decided to return to Bethlehem in Judah and the daughters-in-law resolved to go with her. As they were on their way, Naomi tried to persuade her daughters-in-law to turn back to their own country. Then Orpha kissed Naomi and went back to her own people.

But the other daughter-in-law, whose name was Ruth, would not go. "Do not urge me to leave you or to go back," she said, "for wherever you go I will go, and wherever you stay I will stay; your people shall be my people, and your God my God; I will die where you die and be buried there."

When Naomi saw that Ruth had made up her mind to go with her, she ceased urging her to return. So they traveled on until they came to Bethlehem.

When they arrived there it was the beginning of the barley harvest. In order to support herself and her mother-in-law, Ruth went into the fields to pick up the scattered heads of grain left by the reapers. Guided by the Lord, she went to glean in the fields of Boaz, a man of great wealth. When he saw Ruth and heard how brave and kind she had been to follow Naomi, he spoke kindly to her and let her eat with the reapers. He further commanded his men to treat her with respect and to let fall some of the handfuls of grain on purpose so that she might gather them without being embarrassed.

Ruth told her mother-in-law all this. Naomi said, "The man is of near kin to us." Now there was a law in Israel that if a man died childless, the nearest of kin should take the wife, and the first son of this marriage should be regarded as the son of him who was dead. As soon as Boaz learned of his kinship to Ruth, who was a good woman, he took her for his wife.

And the Lord gave her a son, and they named him Obed; he became the father of Jesse, who was the father of David. Thus Jesus Christ was a descendant of Ruth and Boaz.

CHAPTER FOUR

A GREAT KINGDOM

When Samuel had grown old, the elders of Israel told him that they wanted to have a king instead of a judge. The man chosen was Saul, of the tribe of Benjamin.

Saul laid the foundations for a strong and united nation. After him came David, a great warrior, who increased the territories of Israel and made Jerusalem the capital of the kingdom. He also made it the center of the great religious ceremonies of his people. The Psalms, many of which are said to have been written by David, express the thoughts of Israel at worship. This collection of religious poetry came to be the hymnbook of the Hebrews.

The building of the great Temple fell to Solomon, David's son. King David left to Solomon a country stronger than its neighbors and victorious over all its enemies. Famed for his wisdom and remarkable building, Solomon gave to the Hebrews a great reputation throughout the Eastern world. Visitors came from afar to learn of the wisdom of Solomon and see the grandeur of his kingdom. It was the "golden age" of the temporal power of the Hebrew nation.

But Solomon's ambition and his foreign interests led to a decline in the unity of the nation. Upon his death the kingdom was divided and was never after united again. The nation's great power and prosperity were soon ended.

THE FIRST KING

When Samuel had grown old, he appointed his sons judges over Israel, but they were not upright like their father, nor did they walk in the fear of the Lord. Then the elders of the Israelites asked for a king so that they might be like other nations.

At the command of God, Samuel anointed a young man named Saul to be the king. He was a handsome and valiant young man, from the tribe of Benjamin. When he stood among the people, he was head and shoulders above all the other men of Israel. And Samuel said to the people, "Look now at him whom the Lord has chosen; there is none like him among all the people." And all the people shouted, "God save the king!"

In the beginning of Saul's reign the Lord was with him, and gave him victory over his enemies. But Saul disobeyed the commandments of the Lord. In a war with the Amalekites he kept, contrary to God's command, the best of the spoils. Then Samuel came to him saying, "Why did you not obey the voice of the Lord?" Saul answered that he had intended to sacrifice the best of the spoil to the Lord. But Samuel answered, "To obey is better than sacrifice. Because you have rejected the word of the Lord, he has rejected you from being king." And his sons were forbidden to succeed him.

DAVID, THE HERO

The Lord sent Samuel to Jesse, a Bethlehemite of the tribe of Judah, to anoint one of his sons to become king after Saul. When Samuel saw the oldest of the sons, he said, "Surely this is the Lord's anointed." But the Lord said to Samuel, "Do not look at his appearance or at the height of his stature, for the Lord does not see as man sees; man looks at the outward appearance, but the Lord looks at the heart." Six other sons of Jesse passed before Samuel, but the Lord had not chosen any of them. At the request of Samuel, Jesse then sent for David, his youngest son, who kept the sheep. And the Lord said, "Arise, anoint him! for this is he." Then Samuel took the horn of oil, and anointed him. And the Spirit of the Lord came upon David from that day forward. But the Spirit of the Lord departed from Saul, and an evil spirit troubled him.

War again broke out between the Philistines and the Israelites. The Philistine army was encamped on the side of a mountain, and directly across it on another mountain the Israelites were encamped. Only a narrow valley lay between them. A giant, named Goliath, came forward from the Philistines. He was more than nine feet tall, and when he defied the Israelites to send out a man to battle against him, no one dared to go. For forty days this giant kept calling for an opponent, much to the shame of Saul and the terror of the Israelites.

David had come to the camp to visit his brothers. When he saw Goliath and heard his taunts, his blood boiled within him and he asked, "Who is this Philistine, that he dares to defy the armies of the living God?" He went to Saul and said, "I will fight the giant."

At first Saul refused, but finally answered, "Go, and the Lord be with you." Then Saul put his best armor on David, but David, being unaccustomed

"David and Jonathan made a covenant

to it, took it off; he took his staff in his hand, and choosing five smooth stones for his sling, he went to meet Goliath. When the giant saw him, he was angry. "Do you think I am a dog, seeing you come to fight me with a club?" he asked. David answered, "You come with a sword, a spear, and a shield; I come in the name of the Lord of hosts. All the people shall see that the Lord does not save by sword and spear; for the battle is the Lord's."

Then David took one of the small smooth stones that he carried with him, and, throwing it with his sling, struck the Philistine on the forehead with such force that he fell with his face to the ground. Then David ran and, drawing the sword of Goliath from its sheath, he killed him. When the Philistines saw that their champion was slain, they fled, and the Israelites pursued them and took their camp.

SAUL'S HATRED FOR DAVID

When Saul and his army returned from their victory over the Philistines, the women came out of the different cities playing and singing,

"Saul has killed his thousands,
But David his tens of thousands."

This made Saul very angry, and one day he tried to kill David by hurling a spear at him, but David dodged the spear and escaped.

After this Saul offered his daughter Michal in marriage to David on condition that he would fight the Philistines. In this way Saul planned that the Philistines would slay David in battle. But David came back more of a hero than ever, and this only increased the jealousy that gnawed at Saul's heart.

In proportion as Saul hated David, so Jonathan, the king's son, did love him. David and Jonathan made a covenant with each other to be friends all their lives. Jonathan even reasoned with his father about his hatred of David, and spoke well of all that his friend had done. For a while Saul seemed satisfied, but again he tried to kill David. Again Jonathan pleaded for his friend, but this time Saul became so angry that he drew his sword to kill his own son!

When Jonathan saw this, he went to David and told him what had happened and urged him to flee for his life. Weeping, he sent David away, but begged him never to forget the promises they had made to each other.

68

*"He took away Saul's
spear and flask of water"*

For a while David's life was in constant danger. One day Saul pursued him and his men with three thousand men. Weary, Saul entered a cave to rest, not knowing that David and his men were hiding there. David's men would have killed Saul, but David stopped them. As the king slept, David cut off the skirt of Saul's robe. When Saul rose up and went out of the cave, David cried after him, showing him the skirt of the robe, saying, "Behold, the Lord delivered you today into my hand; but I would not put forth my hand against the Lord's anointed." And Saul wept and said, "You are more righteous than I; for you have rewarded me with good, whereas I have rewarded you with evil." Another time, when Saul was hunting for David, the latter went into Saul's camp while he and all his people were asleep, and took away Saul's spear and flask of water. When Saul saw that David had again spared his life, he said, "I have sinned; return, my son David, for I will harm you no more." But David distrusted Saul, and fled to the land of the Philistines, where he remained one year and four months.

War broke out again between the Philistines and the Israelites. Saul gathered his men and went forth to meet the enemy, but in battle all the men of Israel fled, Jonathan was killed, and Saul was severely wounded. Fearing that he would be captured by the Philistines, Saul killed himself by falling on his own sword. By Saul's sinful death David was free from danger, but he did not rejoice. He knew that Saul had many virtues, and when he heard of the death of Jonathan, he mourned greatly.

69

DAVID BECOMES KING

After Saul's death David was made king of the Israelites. He made Jerusalem his capital, and because of his strong armies and many victories, his fame spread among all the neighboring nations. In turn he subdued the Philistines, the Moabites, the Syrians, the Edomites, and the Ammonites. Great treasures of gold and large quantities of booty were brought to Jerusalem. Before David died he had extended his kingdom as far south as Egypt and as far north and east as the Euphrates River.

David gave much attention to order and justice in his kingdom. He chose wise men for his counselors and upright men to rule over the people. He also had honest men in charge of all his property. His reign was a time of prosperity and good order.

Moreover, David took much interest in spreading the worship of the true God among his subjects. On Mount Zion he erected a tent for the worship of God. In the midst of the shouting of the crowds and the sound of trumpets, he had the ark carried to the place of worship. David himself walked before the priests, playing his harp. And after they had set the ark in the tabernacle, sacrifices of burnt offerings and peace offerings were made to the Lord.

David also appointed certain priests to serve in the sanctuary and conduct services of worship at regular times. The sacred songs that were sung at the services were later collected into the Book of Psalms. From the Levites were chosen four thousand singers whose duty it was to chant, day by day, the praises of God and to play all manner of musical instruments.

When the Lord had given David rest from all his enemies round about, the king said to Nathan, the prophet, "See, now, I dwell in a house of cedar, but the ark of God dwelleth within curtains." Nathan answered, "Thus saith the Lord: Thou shalt not build a house for my name, because thou hast been a man of war. I will set up thy seed after thee; he shall build a house for my name. And thy house and thy kingdom shall be established for ever."

DAVID'S SIN AND REPENTANCE

During one of his wars David sent messengers and took Bath-sheba, the wife of Uriah, one of his officers. She was a beautiful woman and he had fallen in love with her. Then, to make matters worse, he sent Uriah with a letter to Joab, one of his generals, telling him to put Uriah in the front lines where the danger would be greatest. Joab did as the letter commanded, and Uriah was killed in battle. Soon after, David married Bath-sheba.

The thing that David had done displeased the Lord and he sent the prophet Nathan to him. "Why have you despised the word of the Lord," he asked, "and done evil in his sight? Now the sword shall never depart from your house, and I will raise up evil against you out of your own house." David humbly acknowledged his faults and confessed his sins against the Lord. When he repented, God forgave him, but, as a punishment, he did send David many trials.

One of the most severe trials that came to David was the treacherous revolt of his son Absalom. This son was the most handsome man in all Israel. He began to undermine his father by flattering the people and causing them to think that he would be more just and generous toward them as king than his father was.

When he thought he had enough people friendly toward him, he openly revolted and had himself proclaimed king.

When King David heard of it, he fled from Jerusalem. Passing over the brook Kidron, he went up to the Mount of Olives, weeping on the way, and hastened to the country east of the Jordan. Absalom pursued his father beyond the Jordan; the two armies met, and Absalom was defeated. While he fled, mounted on a mule, Absalom passed under a large oak tree. His long hair caught in the branches of the tree, and the mule galloped on, leaving Absalom hanging by his hair. As soon as Joab, one of David's trusted generals, saw him, he thrust a spear into the unthankful heart of Absalom. When David heard of his son's death, he wept and said, "O my son Absalom, would to God that I had died in your stead! Absalom, my son Absalom!"

THE LAST YEARS OF DAVID'S REIGN

When David had grown old, he made Solomon his son king over Israel, for him the Lord had chosen from among the sons of David to rule over his people. And David gathered all the princes of Israel at Jerusalem. In the presence of this assembly, he turned the government over to Solomon, took farewell of all Israel, and said to Solomon, "The Lord has chosen you to build a house for the sanctuary. Be strong and of good courage, and do it;

for the Lord God, even my God, will be with you; he will not fail you, nor forsake you, until you have finished the house of the Lord."

David gave Solomon plans for the temple and its furnishings. David had also prepared for the house of God much gold, silver, precious stones, and building material, and had besides this given of his own property gold and silver. At the request of David, the princes of the people gave freely rich gifts for the house of God. David also warned Solomon that it was not a house for man that he was building, but a dwelling-place for the Lord. He also told his son never to forsake the Lord, but to serve him with a faithful heart, and to remember that in the day he forsook God, God would forsake him. And the people rejoiced, and David blessed the Lord before all the congregation and said, "Thine, O Lord, is the greatness, and the power, and the glory, and the victory, and the majesty; thine is the kingdom, and thou art exalted as head above all."

David died, having reigned forty years, and he was buried on Mount Zion. His son Solomon became king after him.

THE REIGN OF SOLOMON

In the beginning Solomon loved the Lord and walked in his father's footsteps. And Solomon prayed to the Lord for wisdom, so that he might rule with justice. And it pleased the Lord that Solomon had asked for this, and he said, "Because thou hast asked this thing, and not long life, nor riches, behold, I have done according to thy word. So, I have given thee a wise and understanding heart, and I have also given thee that which thou hast not asked, both riches and honor."

And God gave Solomon such wisdom and understanding that he excelled the wisdom of all surrounding nations. Solomon also wrote many songs and proverbs. Some of these are gathered together in the Old Testament Book of Proverbs and the Book of Psalms. He also had great knowledge of plants and animals, the stars and the earth, so that the wise men of the world and the princes of many nations came to hear him.

Solomon had a peaceful reign and all his people lived in safety. His was also a reign of prosperity and his kingdom included more territory than the kingdom of any of the other rulers of the Israelites.

72

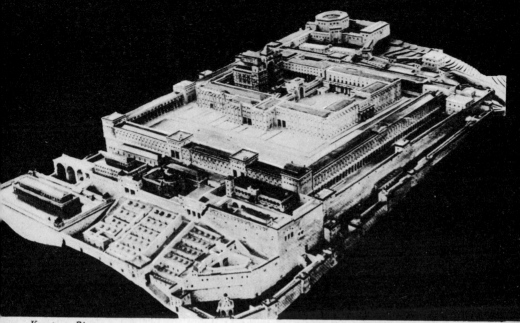

Replica of Solomon's Temple

In the fourth year of Solomon's reign, he began to build the house of the Lord on Mount Moriah. In seven years the glorious temple was completed. Then king Solomon assembled all the elders and the princes of Israel in Jerusalem, to bring up the Ark of the Covenant and all the holy vessels from Zion to the temple. And when the priests had carried the ark into the Most Holy Place, the glory of the Lord filled the house. And Solomon stood before the altar of the Lord in the presence of all the congregation of Israel, and kneeled down, and spread forth his hands toward heaven, and said, "O Lord God of Israel, the heavens cannot contain thee; how much less this house that I have built! May thine eyes be open toward this house night and day, of which thou hast said, My name shall be there. Hearken therefore to the supplications of thy people Israel, which they shall make toward this place; and when thou hearest, forgive. Moreover concerning the stranger that cometh out of a far country, for thy great name's sake, if they come and pray in this house; then hear thou from the heavens; that all people of the earth may know thy name." Thereupon Solomon blessed all the congregation of Israel and said, "The Lord our God be with us, as he was with our fathers, that he may incline our hearts unto him, to walk in all his ways, and to keep

73

his commandments, and his statutes." Great sacrifices were offered before the Lord, and the celebration continued fourteen days. So the king and all Israel dedicated the house of the Lord.

But King Solomon did not end his reign as he began it. When he grew old he was led away from God by many strange women. These wives persuaded him to worship idols and in order to please his women, he built a temple for their idols. Then the Lord was angry with Solomon and said to him, "I will surely rend the kingdom from thee, and will give it unto thy servant. Notwithstanding, in thy days I will not do it for David thy father's sake, but I will rend it out of the hand of thy son."

So Solomon fell from his greatness. Before he died, he had begun to oppress his subjects and disappoint his people until discontent showed itself everywhere. Amid gloom and disappointment, Solomon, once the wisest of men, passed away, a sorry example of the weakness of man and the vanity of life when it is not obedient to God.

THE DIVISION OF THE KINGDOM

After the death of Solomon the people came to his son Rehoboam, the new king, and asked him to make lighter the burden which his father had placed upon them. Rehoboam bade them to return in three days for their answer. He then asked the older men what to do, and they advised him to be kind and merciful; after that he consulted the young men, and they advised him to be severe. Unfortunately Rehoboam took the advice of the young men. When the people returned for their answer he said, "My father put a heavy yoke upon you; but I will make it heavier."

When the people heard this, they became angry, and ten of the tribes of Israel rebelled against the king. They formed a nation of their own, making Jeroboam their king. The two tribes of Judah and Benjamin remained loyal to Rehoboam, and all the priests and Levites living among the ten tribes went to Jerusalem to be loyal to the son of Solomon.

From this time on the Israelites were divided into two separate kingdoms. The kingdom of Judah was to the south. It had Jerusalem for its capital, and was composed mainly of the two tribes of Judah and Benjamin. The Kingdom of Israel was to the north. It had Samaria for its capital, and was made up of the ten tribes who revolted against Rehoboam.

© *Providence Lithograph Co.*

The Temple Dedicated

75

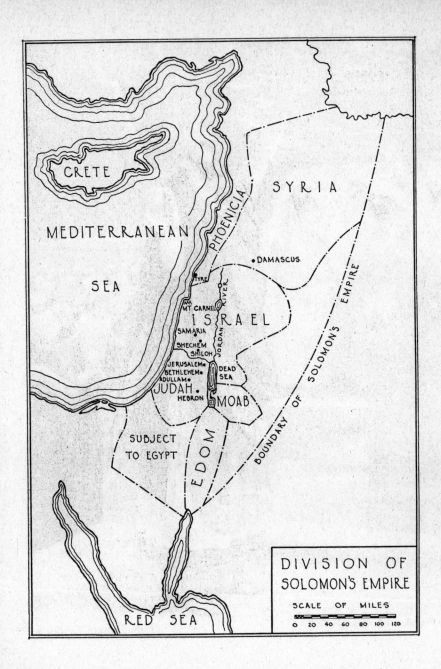

CRETE

MEDITERRANEAN

SEA

SYRIA

PHOENICIA

• DAMASCUS

TYRE

MT CARMEL

ISRAEL

SAMARIA

SHECHEM

SHILOH

JERUSALEM

BETHLEHEM

ADULLAM

JUDAH

HEBRON

JORDAN RIVER

DEAD SEA

MOAB

SUBJECT TO EGYPT

EDOM

BOUNDARY OF SOLOMON'S EMPIRE

RED SEA

DIVISION OF SOLOMON'S EMPIRE

SCALE OF MILES

0 20 40 60 80 100 120

THE KINGDOM OF ISRAEL

After they had separated from the Kingdom of Judah, the people of the Kingdom of Israel began to worship idols. Their king, Jeroboam, was mostly to blame for it, and this is the way he reasoned: "If my people go up to Jerusalem to worship at the temple on the great holidays, as the Law commands, they will soon be friends with the people of Judah and will no longer be loyal to me." So he had calves made of gold, and, setting them up, he said to the people, "These are your gods. Worship them, and do not go up to Jerusalem." The people obeyed and began to worship the idols. And the king made priests of the lowest of the people, who were not of the priestly tribe of Levi.

For about two hundred years the Kingdom of Israel continued to exist as a separate nation. During that time Israel had nineteen kings, most of whom came to the throne by violence. All were like Jeroboam, and not one of them did what was right in the sight of the Lord. It was a time of disorder, vice, and idolatry, and most of the people were no better than their rulers.

To teach and warn both the people and their kings, the Lord raised up a number of godly men called *prophets,* among whom were Elijah, Elisha, Amos, and Hosea. But the people of Israel continued in their wicked ways and paid no attention to the covenant which the Lord had made with their fathers. God did everything to save his chosen people, at one time humbling them at the hands of their enemies, at another cheering them with the promise of the Saviour, but they remained a disobedient people. Finally their kingdom was destroyed by the Assyrians and large numbers of them were led away into captivity in Assyria.

ELIJAH AND THE DROUGHT

Ahab was perhaps the worst of all the kings of Israel. He and his pagan wife Jezebel built a temple to Baal. They appointed four hundred and fifty priests to serve this false god, while at the same time Ahab put to death all the priests of the true God that he could find in his kingdom.

Then the Lord sent Elijah the prophet to tell Ahab that no rain would fall in Israel, and a great famine came which lasted for three years and a half. Ahab became very angry with Elijah and secretly sought to put him to death.

The Lord bade Elijah to go to the brook Cherith. Here ravens brought him food every morning and evening, and from the brook he had water to drink.

After a while the brook dried up; then the Lord told him to go to the city of Zarephath in Zidon, where a widow would feed him. Elijah went, and, as he entered the city, he met a widow from whom he asked for a morsel of bread. She answered, "I have but a handful of meal and a little oil in a cruse." But Elijah answered, "Fear not, for thus saith the Lord God of Israel, the jar of meal shall not be used up nor the oil give out, until the day that the Lord sendeth rain upon the earth." The woman did as he bade her, and her meal was not used up nor did her oil give out.

After three years of famine in the land, Elijah went to Ahab. When the king saw him, he blamed Elijah for the distress that was in the land, but Elijah answered that the distress was the result of the king's idolatry and other sins. "You have forsaken the commandments of the Lord, and followed Baal," he said.

THE CONTEST WITH THE PRIESTS OF BAAL

Then Elijah asked the king to gather together all Israel on Mount Carmel, and also the four hundred and fifty priests of Baal that ate at Queen Jezebel's table. Ahab did so, and went himself to the mountain.

When they were all assembled, Elijah said, "How long will you hesitate between two opinions? If the Lord be God, then follow him, but if Baal, then follow him."

Then Elijah made a proposal: "I am alone; the priests of Baal are four hundred and fifty. Let two bullocks be given us for sacrifice; let the priests of Baal choose one and I will choose the other; let them kill their bullock and I will kill mine; and let each of us lay his bullock on the wood, but put no fire under it; then let them call upon their gods and I will call upon my God, and let the god that answers by fire be God." The people were pleased with the plan.

Then the priests of Baal made ready their bullock upon the altar. From morning till noon they ran around the altar and called upon Baal, but there was no answer. Elijah teased them, saying, "Cry louder; perhaps Baal is asleep, or away on business." They shouted all the louder, and even cut themselves with knives, as was their practice. After noon they raved on till the hour of the evening sacrifice, but there was no answer.

Elijah now bade the people come closer to his altar, and had water poured on the bullock and on the wood. Then he called upon the Lord to show his power, so that the people might be converted. As he prayed, the fire of the Lord fell and consumed the sacrifice. When the people saw it, they fell on their faces and cried out, "The Lord is God; the Lord is God."

According to the Law of Moses, Elijah had all the prophets of Baal put to death, so that they could no longer mislead the people. After this came a plentiful rain.

Queen Jezebel vowed to take the life of Elijah. Therefore he fled to the wilderness of Judah. Here an angel fed him, and strengthened by this food, the prophet went forty days and nights to Horeb, the mount of God. Here he complained before the Lord that Israel had forsaken the covenant of the Lord and that his labor was in vain. And there came a strong wind which rent the mountains, but the Lord was not in the wind, neither was he in the earthquake, nor in the fire; after the fire came the sound of a small voice. Then Elijah wrapped his face in his mantle, and the voice of the Lord spoke to him, "I have seven thousand left in Israel, whose knees have not bowed unto Baal." Thereupon Elijah returned to his own country.

NABOTH'S VINEYARD

A man by the name of Naboth had a vineyard next to the palace of Ahab. The king wished to buy it, but Naboth refused to part with the inheritance of his father. When Ahab came to his house heavy and displeased, Jezebel said to him, "Cheer up. I will get you Naboth's vineyard." So she wrote letters in Ahab's name to the elders of Naboth's city that they should set two men to testify that Naboth had blasphemed God and the king. The elders did as Jezebel had commanded, and Naboth was carried out of the city and stoned to death. No sooner had Ahab taken possession of the land than Elijah met him and said, "Thus saith the Lord: Hast thou killed and also taken possession? In the place where dogs licked the blood of Naboth, shall dogs lick up thine own."

This prophesy was later fulfilled. Ahab fell in battle, and dogs came and licked his blood from the war-chariot in which he had been wounded. Jezebel lived a few years longer, but when Jehu had become king, he ordered her to be thrown down from a window; there horses trod her under foot, and dogs devoured her.

ELIJAH AND ELISHA

At the command of the Lord Elijah anointed Elisha to be prophet in his place. One day as they walked together and talked, there appeared a chariot of fire and horses of fire and Elijah was taken up by a whirlwind into heaven. Elisha saw it and took up the mantle of Elijah that fell from him. And the spirit of Elijah rested upon Elisha, so that he performed many miracles.

NAAMAN

Naaman, who commanded the army of the king of Assyria, was a good man, but he was a leper. Now on one of their raids the Syrians had carried off as a prisoner from the land of Israel a little girl who waited on Naaman's wife. She said to her mistress, "Would that my lord saw the prophet who lives in Samaria, for he would cure my lord of his leprosy!"

So Naaman drove with his horses and chariot and came to the door of the house of Elisha. Then Elisha sent out a messenger to Naaman, saying, "Go and wash in the Jordan seven times, and you shall be well and clean." But Naaman was angry, and went away saying, "I thought he would surely come out to me and call upon the Lord to bless me, waving his hand over the sore places, and cure me. Are not the waters of Damascus better than the waters of Israel?"

But the servants said, "If the prophet had told you to do something difficult, would you not have done it? How much rather then, when he tells you only to wash and be clean?"

At this Naaman went and dipped seven times in the Jordan, and the leprosy left him. Then, returning to the man of God, he offered him a gift, but Elisha would not accept it. And Naaman said, "I will no longer offer sacrifice to other gods, but unto the Lord."

THE DOWNFALL OF THE KINGDOM OF ISRAEL

Although the people of Israel were warned time after time by their spiritual leaders to turn from their sinful ways, they only grew more idolatrous and disobedient. Finally God grew weary of their sins and permitted the destruction of their nation.

Against Israel came Shalmaneser, king of Assyria. King Hoshea became his servant, and agreed to pay tribute each year. Later, however, Hoshea entered into a conspiracy with the king of Egypt against Shalmaneser and did not pay his yearly tribute. Thereupon the king of Assyria came with a powerful army, took Samaria, and carried a large part of the inhabitants back as captives. This was in 722 B. C. And the Lord rejected these people of Israel, so that they never returned from their captivity. Being mixed with the people of Assyria and surrounding nations, they ceased to exist as a nation. No trace of "the ten lost tribes of Israel" now remains.

Furthermore, the king of Assyria brought people from his kingdom and placed them in the cities of Samaria, from which he had taken away many captives. These people mingled with the remnant of the Israelites, and in time they became a mixed race, known as the Samaritans.

The religion of the Samaritans was a mixture of true Judaism and paganism. The Jews in Judea hated their Samaritan neighbors because of their mixed religion as well as their mixed nationality.

View of the Jordan Valley

Philip Gendreau Photo

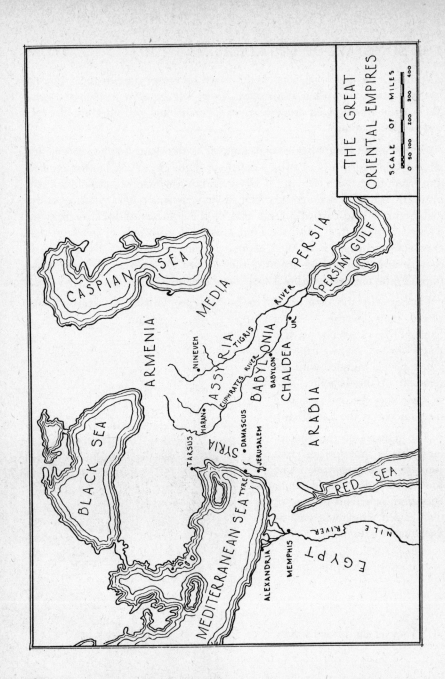

THE GREAT
ORIENTAL EMPIRES

SCALE OF MILES

0 50 100 200 300 400

CASPIAN SEA

ARMENIA

MEDIA

PERSIA

PERSIAN GULF

ASSYRIA

• NINEVEH

TIGRIS RIVER

EUPHRATES RIVER

BABYLONIA

BABYLON•

CHALDEA

UR•

RIVER

ARABIA

• HARAN

SYRIA

TARSUS•

• DAMASCUS

•JERUSALEM

BLACK SEA

TYRE•

MEDITERRANEAN SEA

RED SEA

ALEXANDRIA•

MEMPHIS•

EGYPT

NILE RIVER

82

CHAPTER SIX

THE KINGDOM OF JUDAH

The kingdom of Judah existed for about four hundred years, which was about two hundred years longer than the time of the kingdom of Israel. The people of Judea were not as disobedient toward the Lord, and at times the nation enjoyed peace and prosperity. Some of Judah's kings were wise and just, but many were wicked and unwise. Though several mighty prophets came to plead with them, they gave themselves to idolatry and led the people into sin. The warnings of the prophets against idolatry and unwise alliances with foreign powers often fell on deaf ears.

To punish their waywardness, God permitted Jerusalem to be taken by the Babylonians. The people were carried away into captivity, and the kingdom of Judah was destroyed.

For seventy years the Jews were captives in Babylon. During this time they humbled themselves before God and their faith was strengthened. At the end of the seventy years, the Persians overthrew the Babylonians and permitted the Jews to return to their own country. They rebuilt Jerusalem and its walls and its temple. For two hundred years they lived in peace. After the death of Alexander the Great, 323 years before Christ, they were oppressed by various neighboring nations until some freedom was gained in 165 B. C. under the leadership of a family of patriots, called the Maccabees. For a hundred years the Jews enjoyed this freedom. Then, in 63 B. C., Pompey brought Jerusalem under the power of the Roman Emperor. After this the Emperor chose the rulers of Judea. When Christ was born, his country was under the sway of Emperor Augustus, who had approved the selection of Herod as king of the Jews.

KINGS OF JUDAH

Among the kings of Judah who walked in the ways of the Lord three were outstanding: Jehoshaphat, Hezekiah, and Josiah.

Jehoshaphat

King Jehoshaphat was the best king Judah had had since the best days of Solomon. He tried to abolish idolatry and sent strong leaders from the princes and priests to teach the people the law of God. He also appointed good men to serve as judges in the country, and commanded them to judge in the fear of the Lord. And the Lord was with Jehoshaphat, so that during his reign of twenty-five years his kingdom had peace on all sides.

Hezekiah

After Jehoshaphat came several cruel and idolatrous kings and a queen, named Athalia, the daughter of the hated Ahab; she was almost worse than any of the kings.

Hezekiah, like David, was a man according to God's own heart. He purified the temple and tried to abolish idolatry. God prospered him and enabled him to withstand the Assyrians when they took Israel captive and threatened to do the same to all Judah. Isaiah the prophet was a great help to him.

Josiah

Josiah was only eight years when he became king. In the twelfth year of his reign he commenced to purge Judah and Jerusalem of the worship of idols. During his reign the high priest found in the house of the Lord the lawbook of Moses which had almost become forgotten. And the king made a covenant with all the people before the Lord to keep his commandments and testimonies with all their heart and with all their soul. During his time appeared the prophets Zephaniah and Jeremiah. Josiah reigned thirty-one years, and was one of the best kings spoken of in the Bible.

CAPTIVITY IN BABYLONIA

After the death of Josiah there came several kings who did evil in the sight of the Lord. The prophet Jeremiah declared that the kingdom of Judah would be overthrown by the king of Babylon and that the people would serve him for seventy years. No one would believe it. But Nebuchadnezzar, king of Babylon, came three times and besieged Jerusalem.

The first time he carried away a part of the vessels of the house of the Lord to Babylon and placed them in his own temple; he also carried into captivity several young men of the principal families, among them Daniel. From the time of this conquest is reckoned the Babylonian captivity, which lasted about seventy years.

The second time, he carried away the mighty men of the land, the craftsmen and the smiths; none remained, save the poorest classes of the people of the land. Among the captives was Ezekiel, the priest.

After the last siege Jerusalem was pillaged and destroyed, the temple of the Lord burned and Zedekiah, the last king of Judah, was carried captive to Babylon together with the greater part of the people, and all vessels and treasures from the temple of the Lord. This was in 586 B. C. Jerusalem was now laid waste and Jeremiah the prophet gave expression to his sorrow in his book of Lamentations.

Among the Jews thus carried away false prophets arose who sought to induce the people to revolt against the king of Babylon. The prophet Jeremiah, who remained in the land of Judah, sent a letter to the captives in which he said, "Thus saith the Lord: Seek the peace of the city, whither I have caused you to be carried away captives, and pray unto the Lord for it, for in the peace thereof shall ye have peace. After seventy years I will visit you, and cause you to return to this place. For I know the thoughts that I think toward you, thoughts of peace and not of evil."

In the affairs of this world the captives prospered; nevertheless the pious ones longed eagerly to return to the land of their fathers, to the holy city, and to the divine worship. This longing is expressed in the One Hundred and Thirty-seventh Psalm, especially the words:

> By the rivers of Babylon,
> There we sat down, yea, we wept,
>   When we remembered Zion.
> Upon the willows in the midst thereof
> We hanged up our harps.
>
> For they that carried us away captive required of us a song,
> And they that wasted us required of us mirth, saying,
>   "Sing us one of the songs of Zion."
> How shall we sing the Lord's song
> In a strange land?
>
> If I forget thee, O Jerusalem,
> Let my right hand forget her cunning;
>   Let my tongue cleave to the roof of my mouth,
>   If I remember thee not;
>   If I prefer not Jerusalem above my chief joy.

Among the captives of Babylon the prophet Ezekiel labored, exhorting and comforting his people with the promise of a future deliverance. During this time of deep sorrow the Jewish people learned to know how bad it is to worship strange gods.

DANIEL

Among the captives at Babylon were several young princes of Judah. The brightest and most handsome of these were selected by King Nebuchadnezzar for special training so that they might become useful to him. The food that these young men received was the best in the land, for it came from the king's own table.

However, the Jewish law forbade the eating of certain foods. So Daniel and his three companions from Judah, unwilling to break the rules of their religion, asked for permission to eat simple food instead of the rich food that came from the king's table. "If, after ten days, we are not stronger and healthier than those who eat food from the king's table, we shall submit," they said, and the officer in charge agreed to their proposition.

God was with them, so that when some time afterward they were called before the king, no others were found to equal them in strength and appearance and wisdom. Thus they were selected and placed in high positions of responsibility.

Later, when King Belshazzar once at a great feast became drunk and caused the vessels from the temple at Jerusalem to be brought that he might drink out of them, a human hand was seen writing upon the wall of the king's palace. When none of the wise men of Babylon could read the writing, Daniel was called. He interpreted the writing, saying it meant that the kingdom was to be divided and given to the Medes and Persians. In the same night, Belshazzar, the Chaldean king, was slain and Darius the Median took the kingdom.

Darius made Daniel a prince over a third part of his kingdom. Then this Daniel was preferred above the other officers, and the king thought to set him over the whole realm. The other officers were full of envy, and persuaded the king to decree, that whosoever should ask a petition of any God or man for thirty days, except from the King Darius, should be cast into the den of lions.

But Daniel kneeled upon his knees three times a day and prayed, and gave thanks to his God, as he had done before. Then his enemies accused him before the king. The king was much displeased, but the men said, "The law of the Medes and Persians is: that no decree nor statute which the king makes may be changed."

So the king had Daniel cast into the den of lions and said, "Your God whom you serve continually, he will deliver you." Early the next morning the king

Daniel and his companions refuse to break the rules of their religion

went in haste to the den of lions, where he heard from Daniel, that God had sent his angel to shut the mouths of the lions, so that they had not hurt him, because he believed his God. The king was very glad and commanded that they should take Daniel up out of the den. He further caused the men who had accused Daniel to be cast into the den, and the lions broke all their bones to pieces before they reached the bottom of the den.

And the king wrote to all people in his realm: "I make a decree, that in every dominion of my kingdom men tremble and fear before the God of Daniel: for he is the living God, and steadfast forever; he delivereth and rescueth, and he worketh signs and wonders in heaven and in earth."

Daniel stands out as the greatest hero of the Babylonian captivity. He is the ideal exile, always loyal to the faith of his fathers, no matter how great the cost.

THE JEWS RETURN FROM CAPTIVITY

After the many years of captivity foretold by the prophets were finished, Cyrus of Persia, who had become king of Babylon, issued an edict stating that the Jews might return to Jerusalem and rebuild the temple of the Lord. He also gave back to them the sacred vessels of gold and silver which Nebuchadnezzar had carried away from Jerusalem.

About 536 B. C., more than forty thousand Jews left Babylon and returned to Judea. Their leader was Zerubbabel, a prince of the family of David.

During the second year of their return the people began to rebuild the temple at Jerusalem. The Samaritans offered to help them, but the offer was refused. For twenty-one years the Jews labored on the new building, encouraged by Haggai and Zechariah. When it was finished, the house of the Lord was dedicated with joy and sacrifices, but when the old men came to see it, they wept in disappointment, for its magnificence was nōt to be compared to that of the temple of Solomon.

Ezra, a scribe of priestly order, came to Jerusalem somewhat later, together with a number of other Jews from Babylon. He taught the children the law of the Lord. In the year 445 B. C. Nehemiah was appointed governor in Judea, and under his direction the walls of Jerusalem were rebuilt. Together with Ezra, Nehemiah worked zealously for the restoration of the worship and government according to the law of Moses. During the time of Nehemiah lived Malachi (about 440 B. C.), whose book is placed last in the Old Testament.

CHAPTER SEVEN

THE PROPHETS

We have already spoken of some of the prophets and followed the account of two of them: Elijah and Elisha.

The prophets were men sent from God to teach the people the will of God. They also foretold certain events; for example, the Babylonian captivity as a punishment for the people's sins, and the coming of the Saviour in fulfillment of God's promise to Israel. Thus they were both *fore-tellers,* telling what was going to happen; and *forth-tellers,* speaking for God and declaring the will of God for his people.

The messages of some of the prophets were written down and are now in the Bible, such as Amos, Hosea, Isaiah, and Jeremiah. Others did not write their messages; for instance, Elijah and Elisha did not.

In a short course in Bible history there is not time to take up a thorough study of each prophet who has left a message in the Bible. However, we ought to learn at least the main facts about a few of these good men so that we may then better understand both the work they did and the message they brought the people.

AMOS

Amos was a prophet in Israel. His message is a remarkable plea for justice to the poor. When he appeared in the Northern Kingdom, more than seven hundred years before Christ, the prophets as a class had become selfish and insincere, the rulers of the people were worldly, and the poor were being oppressed. He explained that being a prophet was not really his profession — he was only a poor workingman whom the Lord had called — but he did have the boldness to predict that unless the king and his people repented of their sins, the Northern Kingdom would be destroyed.

The times were prosperous when Amos prophesied. Many people lived in wealth and splendor; a large number of the women were very selfish and pampered ("Fat cows of Bashan," Amos called them.). On the other hand, the poor were being oppressed. Their rights were ignored by corrupt judges, nobles, and priests. The wealthy cheated the poor by using false scales and measures when they sold them food and they underpaid them when they hired them to work by the day. Business men were so absorbed in their business that they could hardly wait for the Sabbath to pass so that they could resume their cheating.

Against these and other wrongs Amos spoke with boldness. God is just and will not be deceived; He rules over all nations, and Israel will be punished for transgression as much as any other people.

To be sure, the people of Israel did not forget their religious services. They made sacrifices, participated in elaborate services of worship, and observed the Sabbath. But they did not let their religion control their lives; cruelty, dishonesty, and selfishness ruled them. This was the worst kind of disobedience to God, for whom Amos speaks, saying:

"I hate, I despise your feasts, and I will take no delight in your solemn assemblies.

Yea, though ye offer me your burnt-offerings and meal-offerings, I will not accept them; neither will I regard the peace-offerings of your fat beasts.

Take thou away from me the noise of thy songs; for I will not hear the melody of thy viols.

But let justice roll down as waters,

And righteousness as a mighty stream."

Thus, we see Amos standing out long before the time of Christ as a heroic messenger of God, waging unceasing war against wrong, no matter how great the cost to himself.

HOSEA

Hosea came upon the scene in the Northern Kingdom only a few years after Amos. The kingdom was at the height of its power, but the people had abandoned the sincere worship of God and obedience toward him. Instead, they were adopting strange religions and living wicked lives.

It was against such unfaithfulness that Hosea preached. To get the people to listen to his message and think of its meaning, he did a sensational thing. Hosea told them the story of his own unhappy married life and

*"The Prophets spoke
against cheating the poor"*

COPR. BY PROVIDENCE LITHOGRAPH CO.

the wickedness of his wife, whose name was Gomer. She had left him to go with other men. Finally he found her in a slave market, forsaken by the men who had pretended to love her. Though she surely did not deserve it, Hosea bought her freedom and took her back home to be his wife.

Israel, said Hosea, is no better than Gomer was. Israel has been unfaithful to God, and has forsaken him in order to love and serve strange gods. There is no honesty, kindness, or knowledge of God among the people. But just as Hosea was patient and forgiving toward his undeserving wife, so the Lord has been full of mercy toward Israel. He cannot give her up! He will not punish, but will forgive.

As Amos is the prophet of justice, so Hosea stands out as the messenger of the forgiving love of God.

ISAIAH

In the year that King Uzziah died (about 740 B. C.), a young aristocrat in Jerusalem had a strange vision. He saw God in all his holiness, and, falling down in awe to worship him, was commanded to go and preach repentance to a disobedient and hard-hearted people.

At first the task seemed hopeless, but Isaiah went. Though the people were prosperous, it was a difficult time in the Kingdom of Judah, for the Assyrians were threatening to occupy their country. Being a member of one of the leading families of the nation, Isaiah tried to influence the king to choose to follow the will of God. He also denounced the sins of the nation —

idolatry, superstition, bribery, injustice, and too much luxury — and he warned that because of them God would destroy the nation.

The book of Isaiah is rich in prophecies concerning Christ and his work; because of this he has been called the gospel preacher of the Old Testament. Among his prophecies is the one that is often repeated at Christmas:

> "For unto us a child is born, unto us a son is given; and the government shall be upon his shoulders; and his name shall be called Wonderful, Counsellor, Mighty God, Everlasting Father, Prince of Peace."

The latter part of the book of Isaiah seems to have a different setting from that in which Isaiah lived. It is therefore thought by many scholars that another prophet wrote these chapters, in which we also find prophecies of Christ and his work, such as:

> "Surely he hath borne our griefs, and carried our sorrows; yet we did esteem him stricken, smitten of God, and afflicted.
>
> But he was wounded for our transgressions, he was bruised for our iniquities; the chastisement of our peace was upon him and with his stripes we are healed.
>
> All we like sheep have gone astray; we have turned everyone to his own way; and the Lord hath laid on him the iniquity of us all."

JEREMIAH

Jeremiah appeared first in the time of Josiah, ruler of the Southern Kingdom. (See page 84.) From the north trouble was threatening. Some day the Babylonians would come to carry away most of the nation into captivity. This, Jeremiah declared, would be the just punishment of God upon the people for their idolatry and wickedness.

Of course that kind of prophecy made Jeremiah very unpopular. Even the priests were against him. But Jeremiah continued his work with courage and determination. One time he was imprisoned and put in the stocks. Again, he was lowered into a cistern and left to die, but through the efforts of an officer from Ethiopia with the help of a rope his life was saved.

Jeremiah lived to see the second capture of Jerusalem and the destruction of the Temple by the Babylonians. Later he was forced to go to Egypt and there is a tradition that here he met a martyr's death at the hands of his own countrymen.

Jeremiah's message was full of gloom and he himself was known as a very sad and complaining man. He knew that his task was hard and thankless, but he did carry on with heroism and gave the people a message of the power of God to help them in the time of national disaster. Not even the destruction of Solomon's magnificent temple, the pride of every Jew, could destroy the faith that was in the hearts of those who put their trust in the Lord.

Jeremiah should also be remembered because he taught with great earnestness that religion is an individual matter. Each of us is directly accountable to God, no matter what his family or nation have been. Each of us may have the inner life with God which does not perish even though the life of our nation crumbles and temples made with hands are destroyed.

JONAH

The Book of Jonah may be regarded as a great call to foreign missions. The story it tells makes it very clear that the love of God is for all people, and not limited to any one nation. It also shows that there is a better way of getting along with rival or enemy nations than by hating them and fighting them. These were important lessons for the Hebrew nation to learn, for they seem to have had the idea that since they were the descendants of Abraham, therefore they alone were to enjoy the blessings of God's grace. The story of Jonah corrects this wrong idea.

Nineveh, the capital of Assyria, was a very large and populous city. Its people did not worship God, but clung to idols.

To Jonah the Word of the Lord came, bidding him go to Nineveh and preach to its people so that these Gentiles would turn from their wickedness. But Jonah did not want to go on this mission; instead he tried to flee from the presence of the Lord by going to sea. Then the Lord sent out a great wind, so that the ship was ready to go to pieces. The mariners cried every man to his god, and cast into the sea the cargo that was in the ship so as to lighten it. Turning to Jonah, the shipmaster said, "Arise, call upon your God." And the seamen cast lots to know on whose account this evil had come upon them, and the lot fell upon Jonah. He confessed his disobedience and advised them to cast him into the sea. They did so, and the storm ceased.

But the Lord had prepared a big fish to swallow up Jonah, and he was in the belly of the fish three days and three nights. Then Jonah cried to the Lord in his anguish, and the Lord heard his voice and caused the fish to throw up Jonah on to dry land.

For the second time the Lord said to Jonah, "Go to Nineveh and preach to it the preaching that I bid thee." This time Jonah obeyed. He went into Nineveh and brought the message of the Lord to its multitudes. The people believed God, and the king proclaimed a general fast, urging all the people to cry mightily to God so that he would spare their city. When God saw that people turned to him, he heard their prayer and did not destroy the city.

Jonah was displeased because God did not punish Nineveh, as he had warned. Instead of being glad that his message had been believed, Jonah began to sulk. He made himself a booth outside of the city from which he might watch, still thinking that disaster would come to the city. And the Lord caused a gourd to grow, the thick green foliage of which gave Jonah shade from the hot sun, and he was very glad for this vine. But a worm cut the vine so that it withered. And the sun beat upon Jonah's head so that he grew faint and wished that he might die. Then God gave him a great lesson in love and mercy, saying, "Thou art grieved because of the gourd for which thou has not labored; should not I spare Nineveh, that great city in which there are more than a hundred and twenty thousand men?"

This gospel message of God's love makes the Book of Jonah one of the most precious pieces of literature ever written.

A Wall of Jerusalem,
Dating Back to
Old Testament Times

Philip Gendreau Photo

CHAPTER EIGHT

WISDOM AND DEVOTIONAL WRITINGS

No summary of the history of the Hebrew people would be complete without some reference to their literature. In the Old Testament we have not only a record of important events in the history of this nation before the coming of Christ, together with the written messages of their prophets, but also a group of five books that are called *The Writings*. These include the following: Psalms, Proverbs, Job, Ecclesiastes, and the Song of Solomon. They tell us not so much of what people did as of what they thought and how they prayed. Some parts are in the form of prose, while others are in the form of poetry. They show not only clear insight into the truth, but also great beauty of expression

PROVERBS

Among the Hebrews there were not only priests and prophets, but also Wise Men, or teachers whose work it was to instruct the people in both worldly wisdom and religious truth.

Many of their teachings have been handed down to us in the form of proverbs. Of course every people has its proverbs, such as:

"Honesty is the best policy."

"Where there is a will, there is a way."

"Haste makes waste."

Proverbs like these spring out of practical experience and live on the lips of the common people. But among the Hebrews there was an interest in proverbs that is unique. They did more than use them as brief sayings in conversation; they worked them into a system of instruction. The composing of proverbs was cultivated as an art, and at about the time of the exile the Wise Men, who studied the old proverbs and wrote new ones, became the professional teachers of Jewish youth.

In the Bible there is a book called Proverbs. Many of these proverbs are sayings of King Solomon, whose reputation for wisdom had spread far. However, not all of these proverbs originated with Solomon. Other men also made their contribution to this collection of wise sayings.

The underlying idea of the book is expressed in the saying that "The fear of the Lord is the beginning of wisdom." Religion is the cornerstone of life. Obedience to the will of God is the greatest wisdom. The religious life is, after all, the good life.

Some samples of this interesting collection of wisdom show the rich quality of the book:

> "A soft answer turneth away wrath:
>   But a grievous word stirreth up anger . . .
> "As a jewel of gold in a swine's snout,
>   So is a fair woman that is without discretion . . .
> "Better is a dinner of herbs where love is,
>   Than the best of beef and hatred therewith . . .
> "Pride goeth before destruction,
>   And a haughty spirit before a fall . . .
> "Righteousness exalteth a nation:
>   But sin is a reproach to any people."

ECCLESIASTES

This is in many respects a very gloomy book. "Vanity of vanities, saith the preacher; vanity of vanities, all is vanity." That is the way it begins, and it goes on mostly in the same strain. The author finds the world a very dreary place. Friendship and love, art and learning, pleasure and wealth give him little satisfaction. Nothing seems to happen that is worth happening, "and there is no new thing under the sun."

But amid the gloom there is some light. The author has not lost hope. Having faith in God, he believes that God rules the world. Having tasted pleasure, success, wisdom, and other things that men consider good, he comes at last to see that the best thing in life is to fear God and keep his commandments.

THE SONG OF SOLOMON

This is a love story, written in poetic form, and has been regarded as picturing the love of God toward his chosen people. Some scholars, however, look upon it as an expression of true human love whose purpose is to exalt purity of life. The ideals which it upholds are ideals which every nation and family must follow, or sad results are sure to come.

THE PSALMS

The Book of Psalms may be regarded as the hymnbook and prayerbook of the Jewish people. It is a great collection of lyric religious poetry. It was compiled from the work of many writers, and it covers many generations in the history of Israel.

In one respect Hebrew poetry differs greatly from our poetry. It makes no effort to make the lines rhyme. Its style is known as parallelism, in which a second line echoes the thought of the first line by repeating it in other words. An example of this parallelism is found in Psalm 103.8:

"The Lord is merciful and gracious,
Slow to anger and plenteous in mercy."

In Psalm 27 we have another example:

"The Lord is my light and my salvation;
whom then shall I fear?
The Lord is the strength of my life;
of whom then shall I be afraid?"

Some of the psalms are poems of religious meditation. Others are outbursts of spiritual joy. Still others throb with the deep music of penitence and confession of sins. Some of the psalms have to do with individuals, while some of them have to do with the nation. One can hardly imagine a situation in life in which a person would not be able to find in the Psalms suitable words to express his condition. The one way to appreciate the power and beauty of this book is to use it constantly, for of it one can truly say, "The psalms are a mirror in which each man sees the motions of his own soul."

JOB

In the books of Old Testament writings one more remains to be mentioned, and it is regarded by some students as the greatest of all. It is the dramatic poem of Job.

In Old Testament times it was generally believed that happiness and sorrow were measured out to each man as he deserved. If he were good, then he would have a happy time of it. If he were evil, he would be punished. In a general way this is true; but people of long ago, like many in modern times, made the mistake of thinking that if a man were prosperous, it was a sure sign that he stood high in God's favor, while if disasters came upon him, it meant that he

had sinned and that he was being punished. The dramatic story of Job corrects this idea, and shows that a good man may have more sorrows than a wicked man.

Outside of Palestine, in the land of Uz, there lived a good man whose name was Job. He had seven sons and three daughters; besides, he had great wealth in sheep, camels, cattle, and servants.

One day Satan came to the Lord and said that it was easy for a man like Job to serve God because he was rich and successful in all he did. "Touch him with hardship," said Satan, "and he will deny thee and forsake thee." Then God gave Satan permission to cause him all kinds of trouble, only he must not touch Job himself.

Soon after this a messenger came to Job bringing him word that his servants had been slain by the enemy. Then another messenger came to report that fire from heaven had destroyed his sheep. A third reported that other enemies had taken his camels. Last of all, a fourth messenger came with the sad news that the house in which his children were feasting had been blown down by the storm and all were killed.

When Job heard these things he was distressed, but he bowed down and worshipped God saying, "The Lord gave, and the Lord hath taken away; blessed be the name of the Lord." So Job remained faithful to his God and did not sin against him.

Again Satan appeared before the Lord and said that if he would only touch Job himself, this pious man would soon curse the Lord. Then God put Job in Satan's power, only he must spare his life.

So Satan covered Job with boils from head to foot, and he suffered terribly from the pain. Then Job's wife told him it was foolish to believe in God. "Curse God, and die," she said. But Job answered, "What? If we receive good at the hand of God, why shall we not also receive evil?" So again, Job remained faithful to his God.

When Job's friends heard what had befallen him, three of them came to comfort him. At the sight of him, they wept, and sitting down, for seven days and seven nights none of them spoke a word to him. Then Job broke the silence and cursed the day on which he was born.

After that Job's friends began to accuse him, saying that such suffering must be the result of many sins; for they supposed that God always gives health and prosperity to the godly, while he sends sorrow and suffering to the ungodly. But Job answered them that they were miserable comforters. He admitted that though he was not perfect, yet he was not a wicked and deceitful man, and he could not understand why God sometimes permitted the ungodly to prosper while the godly were permitted to suffer. But Job still believed in God and he hoped that the sufferings of the righteous would finally come to an end and that there would be a happy life hereafter. Thus he said,

> "I know that my Redeemer liveth,
> And at the last day he will stand up upon the earth;
> And after my skin, even this body, is destroyed,
> Then without my flesh shall I see God."

Job's confidence in God was not misplaced, for he was finally relieved of his affliction, and God gave him twice as many possessions as he had before.

* * * * * *

The Book of Job is forty-two chapters long. The form in which it is written is much like a drama. It is largely a discussion of the problem of suffering in human life, and its message corrects the idea that disaster and misfortune are always a sign of God's disapproval of one's life while health and prosperity are always a reward for good conduct. The story of Job is one of encouragement to the many godly and upright people who are overtaken by sorrow and suffering. He who believes in God does not expect to have an explanation for everything, but continues to trust in the love of God in both prosperity and adversity.

The Jews Between the Old Testament and the New

SECULAR GOVERNMENT

After the return from Babylon the Jews lived in peace under Persian rule for about two hundred years. Then came Alexander the Great from Macedonia, in the southeastern part of Europe, and overthrew the Persian Empire. After his death, 323 B.C., the Jews were oppressed part of the time by the Egyptians and part of the time by the kings of Syria.

One of these Syrian kings, Antiochus Epiphanes, treated the Jews with great harshness. He robbed their temple of its sacred vessels and set up a statue of Jupiter in the Holy of Holies. He also enraged the people by tearing down the walls of Jerusalem, commanding the sacrifice of swine and destroying all the sacred books that could be found. Because of these outrages the people rose up in revolt under the leadership of Judas Maccabee, a brave and energetic patriot. The Syrian oppression was broken (163 B.C.), and for almost a hundred years the Jews enjoyed some independence.

In the year 63 B.C., Judea became subject to Rome, being taken by Pompey after he had reduced the power of all rulers in Asia Minor. The Jews were required to pay tribute to Rome, but were permitted for a while to choose their own rulers. Augustus was the Emperor at Rome at the time of the birth of Christ, and Herod was king of Judea under Roman sovereignty.

THE GREAT COUNCIL

After the return from captivity the Jews established an ecclesiastical (religious) Council, called the Sanhedrin. It consisted of seventy members, with the high priest as chairman. This Council was the highest governing and judiciary body under Jewish law. It had the general administration of government and of justice, and even had the power to inflict capital punishment. This power, however, was taken from the Council when the Romans conquered Judea.

JEWISH SECTS

During the time of Judas Maccabee two strong sects arose among the Jews: the Sadducees and the Pharisees.

The Pharisees were very strict. They were opposed to alliances with other nations and tried hard to keep their nation strictly Jewish. They made much of the tradition of the elders and observed very religiously the ceremonies of Judaism. Too often, however, they were more interested in outward form than in true godliness, and many became hypocrites. Jesus said of them, "This people honoreth me with their lips, while their heart is far from me."

The Sadducees had no respect for the teachings of the elders, and they denied the resurrection of the body. Most of them lived in worldly enjoyment. Their number was not large, but they were rich and powerful. The high priest and his family belonged to this sect.

It must not be forgotten, however, that among the Jews there were many devout people who were looking for the coming of the promised Saviour.

THE SYNAGOGUE

In the New Testament there is frequent mention of the synagogue. Synagogues were Jewish meeting-houses. They probably came into being among the Jews in the Babylonian captivity. It seems that at that time many of the more devout Jews, far from their native land, felt the need for a place where they could gather, especially on the Sabbath and on feast-days, to hear the Word of God and to worship. The fact that their temple at Jerusalem lay in ruins must have deepened their feeling of need for a house of worship where they lived.

At the time of Jesus synagogues were found in nearly all small towns of Palestine. Jews in cities outside of Palestine also had their synagogues.

The synagogue was shaped much like the small church of today. At one end was the holy chest, or ark, containing the scrolls of the Law and the prophets. These scrolls were long sheets of parchment or papyrus, rolled up at either end on a carefully-made wooden rod. On them the Law and the messages of the prophets were copied with painstaking care.

In front of the ark, and facing the congregation, were the "chief seats" for the officers of the synagogue and wealthy or learned men. The pulpit or desk from which the Scriptures were read was in the middle of the building. When a leader read the Scriptures he stood up, but sat down while he preached or explained the lesson. The place for women and children was separated from the pews or seats where the men sat.

The synagogue was not only a house of worship. It served also as a school and a courthouse. For a person to be cast out of the synagogue meant that he lost both his rights as a member of the religious group and also many of his rights as a citizen of the community.

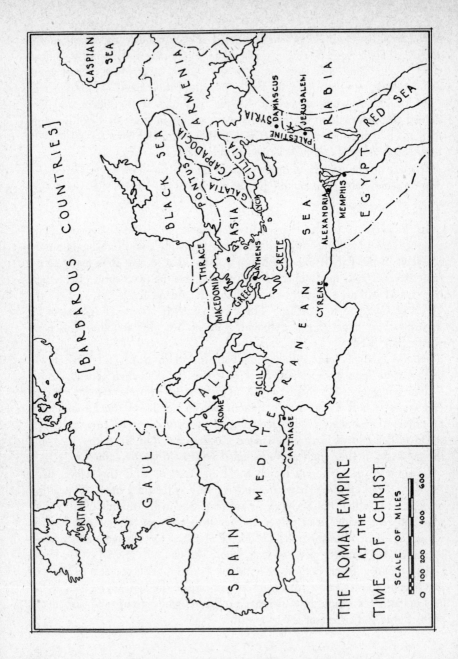

CASPIAN SEA

[BARBAROUS COUNTRIES]

BLACK SEA

ARMENIA

PONTUS

CAPPADOCIA

GALATIA

CILICIA

SYRIA

DAMASCUS

JERUSALEM

PALESTINE

ARABIA

RED SEA

THRACE

ASIA

MACEDONIA

GREECE

ATHENS

CRETE

MEDITERRANEAN SEA

ALEXANDRIA

MEMPHIS

EGYPT

CYRENE

ITALY

ROME

SICILY

CARTHAGE

GAUL

BRITAIN

SPAIN

THE ROMAN EMPIRE
AT THE
TIME OF CHRIST

SCALE OF MILES

0 100 200   400   600

Part II

THE NEW TESTAMENT

CHAPTER ONE

THE BIRTH OF JOHN THE BAPTIST

When Herod was king of Judea there was a priest whose name was Zacharias. The name of his wife was Elizabeth. Both lived godly lives and they blamelessly kept all the commandments of the Lord. But they had no children. They had often asked for a son, but their prayers seemed unanswered. Now both were old.

One day when Zacharias was serving as a priest before God it became his duty to enter into the sanctuary and burn incense while the congregation remained outside the sanctuary and prayed.

Suddenly an angel appeared at the right of the altar. Zacharias was frightened, but the angel bade him not to be afraid. Then the angel told him his prayer had at length been heard.

"Thy wife Elizabeth shall bear thee a son," said the angel, "and thou shalt call his name John. Thou shalt have joy and gladness; and many shall rejoice at his birth. He shall be great in the sight of the Lord, and he shall be filled with the Holy Spirit. He shall turn many of the children of Israel to the Lord their God. He shall go before him in the spirit and power of Elijah, to make ready for the Lord a people prepared for him."

When Zacharias heard this he began to doubt and to say that both he and his wife were too old to have children. In answer to his objection the angel said, "I am Gabriel. I stand in the very presence of God; and I was sent to bring thee these good tidings. Behold, thou shalt be silent and not able to speak, until the day that these things come to pass, because thou didst not believe my words."

When Zacharias came out, he was unable to speak, and the congregation realized that he had seen a vision. He continued making signs to them, and remained speechless. When the time of his service was ended, he went back to his home.

When the time came, Elizabeth gave birth to a son. Her neighbors and her relatives rejoiced with her.

It was customary among the Jews to give a name to a child at his circumcision. The neighbors and relatives wanted to call the baby by his father's name. Then his mother told them, "He shall be called John." "But none of your kin is called by that name," they said.

Then they turned to the father and asked him. Being unable to speak, he took a pen and tablet and wrote, "His name is John."

At this very instant Zacharias was again able to speak, and he began to praise God.

Fear came upon all when they saw and heard what had happened. Soon the news of it spread throughout the hill country of Judea. "What then shall this child be?" they asked. For the hand of the Lord was with him.

The child grew, and the Spirit of the Lord was in him. At an early age he began to spend hours and days in the wilderness not far from his home. Finally he stayed in the wilderness all the time alone with God.

*Ruins of an
Ancient
Synagogue
at Capernaum*

*Philip Gendreau
Photo*

CHAPTER TWO

THE BIRTH AND EARLY LIFE OF JESUS

THE PROMISE

About six months after the angel appeared to Zacharias, he was sent to Nazareth, a little town in Galilee, to a virgin named Mary. She was engaged to be married to a carpenter named Joseph.

Suddenly the angel entered into Mary's room and said, "Hail, thou that art highly favored! The Lord is with thee."

Mary was greatly startled at his words, and wondered what the greeting meant. But the angel said, "Fear not, Mary, for thou hast found favor with God. And thou shalt bring forth a son and shalt call his name JESUS.

He shall be great, and shall be called the Son of the Most High:

And the Lord God shall give unto him the throne of his father David:

And he shall reign over the house of Jacob for ever;

And of his kingdom there shall be no end."

Mary said to the angel, "How shall this be?" And the angel said, "The Holy Spirit shall come upon thee, and the power of the Most High shall

Nazareth, a Little Town in Galilee

Underwood and Underwood Photo

"She laid him in a manger"

overshadow thee: wherefore thy child shall be called the Son of God; for with God nothing is impossible."

And Mary said, "Behold, I am the handmaid of the Lord; let it be to me according to thy word." And the angel left her.

After this the angel of the Lord appeared to Joseph in a dream and said, "Joseph, son of David, Fear not to take Mary to be thy wife. She shall give birth to a son, and thou shalt call his name Jesus, for it is he that shall save his people from their sins."

Joseph did as the angel of the Lord commanded him.

THE BIRTH OF JESUS

There went out a decree from Caesar Augustus that all the world should be taxed. And all went to be taxed, every one in his own city. And Joseph also went up from Galilee, out of the city of Nazareth, to Judea, into the City of David which is called Bethlehem, for he was of the house and lineage of David, to be taxed with Mary his wife. While they were there, Mary gave birth to her first-born son, and wrapped him in swaddling clothes, and laid him in a manger, because there was no room for them in the inn.

And there were in the same county shepherds abiding in the field, keeping watch over their flock by night. Suddenly an angel of the Lord came to them, and the glory of the Lord shone round about them, and they were filled with fear. But the angel said to them, "Fear not: for, behold, I bring you good tidings of great joy, which shall be to all people. For unto you is born this day, in the city of David a Saviour, who is Christ the Lord. And this shall be a sign unto you: ye shall find the babe wrapped in swaddling clothes, lying in a manger." And suddenly there was with the angel a multitude of the heavenly host, praising God and saying: "Glory to God in the highest, and on earth peace, good will toward men."

When the angels had left them and returned to heaven the shepherds went with haste, and found Mary and Joseph, and the babe lying in a manger. And when they had seen it, they told others what had been said to them concerning this child. And all they that heard it were astonished. But Mary kept all these things, pondering them in her heart. And the shepherds returned, glorifying and praising God for all that they had seen and heard, as it had been told them.

PRESENTED IN THE TEMPLE

When eight days had passed the Christ-child was circumcized, according to the religious custom of the Jews, and his name was called Jesus, as the angel had told Mary.

Forty days after the birth of Jesus, they brought him to Jerusalem, to present him to the Lord (Num. 8:16-18; 18:15, 16), and to offer a sacrifice according to the law of the Lord, a pair of turtle doves, or two young pigeons (Lev. 12:18).

In Jerusalem lived a man whose name was Simeon. He was an upright and devout man who was waiting for the consolation of Israel. To him it had been revealed by the Holy Spirit that he should not see death before he had seen the Lord's Christ. And when the parents brought in the child Jesus, he was in the temple. Seeing them, he took the child in his arms, and blessed God, saying:

"Lord, now lettest thou thy servant depart in peace according to thy word; for mine eyes have seen thy salvation, which thou hast prepared before the face of all people, a light to lighten the Gentiles, and the glory of thy people Israel."

Simeon

Joseph and Mary marveled at the things which were spoken of him. And Simeon blessed them, and said to Mary his mother, "Behold, this child is set for the fall and rising again of many in Israel, and for a sign which shall be spoken against. Yea, a sword shall pierce through thine own soul also, that the thoughts of many hearts may be revealed."

There was also Anna, a prophetess, a widow more than eighty years old, who remained at the temple, serving God with fastings and prayers night and

110

day. Coming in just at that moment she also gave thanks to the Lord, and spoke about the child to all who looked for redemption in Jerusalem.

THE WISE-MEN FROM THE EAST

When Jesus was born in Bethlehem of Judea, there came wise-men from the East to Jerusalem, saying, "Where is he that is born King of the Jews? For we have seen his star in the east, and have come to worship him."

When Herod the king heard this, he was greatly disturbed, and all Jerusalem with him. And he called the chief priests and the scribes together and demanded of them where Christ should be born. They said, "In Bethlehem of Judea, for thus it is written by the prophet" (Micah 5:2). Then Herod secretly called the wise-men, and inquired of them what time the star appeared. And he sent them to Bethlehem, saying, "Go and search diligently for the young child, and when you have found him, bring me word again, that I may come and worship him also."

When they had heard the king, they went away, and lo, the star which they saw in the east went before them, till it came and stood over where the young child was. When they saw the star, they rejoiced greatly, and went into the house, and saw the young child with Mary his mother, and fell down and worshipped him. When they had opened their treasures, they presented to him gifts: gold, frankincense, and myrrh. And being warned by God in a dream that they should not return to Herod, they went back to their own country another way.

THE WISE-MEN FROM THE EAST

When the wise-men had departed, the angel of the Lord appeared to Joseph in a dream, saying, "Arise, and take the young child and his mother, and flee into Egypt. Remain there until I bring you word, for Herod will make search for the young child so that he may destroy him." When he arose, he took the child and his mother by night, and went to Egypt. Here they remained until the death of Herod.

When Herod saw that the wise-men had not done as he had asked them, he was very angry, and gave orders to kill all the children that were in Bethlehem and in all its neighborhood, from two years old and under.

But when Herod was dead, an angel of the Lord appeared in a dream to Joseph in Egypt, saying, "Rise, and take the young child and his mother,

"There came wise-men from the East"

112

and go into the land of Israel, for those who were seeking the young child's life are dead." And he rose, and took the young child and his mother, and went to the land of Israel. Here he settled in a town called Nazareth.

The child grew and became strong and full of wisdom, and the grace of God was upon him.

JESUS IN THE TEMPLE AT TWELVE YEARS OF AGE

The parents of Jesus went to Jerusalem every year at the feast of the pass-over. When he was twelve years old, they went up to Jerusalem as was customary at the time of the feast. When they had stayed the full number of days, they started for home, but the child Jesus remained behind in Jerusalem. Joseph and his mother did not know of this, but supposing him to be in the company, they proceeded a day's journey. Then they searched for him among their kinsfolk and acquaintance. When they could not find him, they turned back again to Jerusalem, anxiously looking for him.

After three days they found him in the temple, sitting among the rabbis, both listening to them and asking them questions. And all who heard him were amazed at his understanding and the answers he gave. When they saw him, they were astonished, and his mother said to him, "Son, why hast thou thus dealt with us? Thy father and I have sought thee sorrowing." And he said to them, "How is it that ye sought me? Did ye not know that I must be about my Father's business?"

And he went down with them, and came to Nazareth, and was obedient to them; but his mother kept all these sayings in her heart. And Jesus increased in wisdom and stature, and in favor with God and man.

"Jesus was obedient to his parents"

© *Providence Lithograph Co.*   *"Repent, for the kingdom of heaven is at hand"*

CHAPTER THREE

THE BEGINNING OF THE MINISTRY OF JESUS

PREPARING THE WAY

When Pontius Pilate was Roman governor of Judea, the call of God came to John the son of Zacharias. He obeyed the call and went into the country along the Jordan to preach to the people. The fame of his preaching spread far, and large numbers of people from Jerusalem and Judea came out to hear him. It was of John the Baptist that Isaiah the Prophet spoke, saying, "The voice of one crying in the wilderness, prepare ye the way of the Lord."

"Repent! for the kingdom of heaven is at hand," was the message of this stern man who wore coarse clothing of camel's hair, fastened with a leather girdle round his waist, and whose food was locusts and wild honey.

When the people heard the preaching of John, many of them were deeply stirred and were baptized by him in the Jordan, making open confession of their sins.

John the Baptist made a great impression on the people, and many of them began to wonder if he was not the promised Christ. But John answered, "I indeed baptize you with water, but one mightier than I is coming, whose sandal-strings I am not worthy to untie." By this he meant that he was but the servant of Christ, sent to prepare the way for Him.

JESUS BAPTIZED AND TEMPTED

When Jesus was about thirty years of age, he came from Galilee to the Jordan to be baptized by John. But John would have prevented him, saying, "I need to be baptized of thee, and comest thou to me?" Jesus answered, "Let it be so now, for thus it is fitting for us to fulfill all righteousness." Then he consented, and Jesus was baptized.

When Jesus came up from the water, the heavens were opened, and the Holy Spirit descended upon him like a dove, and a voice came from heaven, saying, "This is my beloved Son, with whom I am well pleased."

Immediately after his baptism, Jesus was led by the Spirit into the wilderness to be tempted by the devil.

When he had fasted forty days and forty nights, he became hungry. And

*"After his baptism Jesus was led by the Spirit
into the wilderness to be tempted"*

116

the tempter came to him and said, "If thou be the Son of God, command these stones to become loaves of bread." But Jesus said, "It is written: Man shall not live by bread alone, but by every word that proceeds from the mouth of God" (Deut. 8:3).

Then the devil took him up into the holy city, and had him stand on a pinnacle of the temple, and said, "If thou be the Son of God, cast thyself down, for it is written:

> He shall give his angels charge of thee, and in their hands they
> shall bear thee up, lest thou strike thy foot against a stone"
> (Ps. 91:11-12).

Jesus said to him, "It is written again: Thou shalt not tempt the Lord thy God" (Deut. 6.16).

Again the devil took him up to the top of a very high mountain, and showed him all the kingdoms of the world and the glory of them, and he said to him, "All these things I will give thee, if thou wilt fall down and worship me." Jesus answered him, "Begone, Satan! for it is written: Thou shalt worship the Lord thy God, and him only shalt thou serve" (Deut. 10:20).

Then the devil left him, and angels came and ministered to him.

THE FIRST DISCIPLES

One day not long after John had baptized Jesus in the Jordan, he saw the Master coming toward him and he said, "Behold, the Lamb of God, that taketh away the sin of the world! This is he of whom I said: After me cometh a man who is before me. . . . And I have borne witness that this is the Son of God."

Again, the next day John was standing with two of his disciples when he saw Jesus passing by, and he said, "Behold, the Lamb of God!" And the two disciples followed Jesus. Andrew was one of the two. He first found his brother Simon and said to him, "We have found the Messiah" (which means Christ). And he brought him to Jesus. When Jesus saw him, he said, "Thou art Simon, the son of Jona, thou shalt be called Cephas" (which means Peter, that is, Rock).

The day following, having decided to leave for Galilee, Jesus found Philip and said to him, "Follow me." Philip found Nathaniel and brought him to Jesus. Jesus saw Nathaniel coming and said of him, "Here is a true Israelite in whom there is no guile." "How dost thou know me?" he asked.

Jesus answered, "Before Philip called thee, when thou wast under the fig tree, I saw thee." Nathaniel said to him, "Rabbi, thou art the Son of God, thou art the King of Israel."

THE FIRST MIRACLE

There was a marriage in Cana of Galilee. Jesus was invited to the feast, as were also his mother and his newly-chosen disciples.

During the feast the wine ran short. Then the mother of Jesus told him, "They have no wine."

Now there were six water-jars of stone standing there (for the Jewish ceremonies of purification), each holding twenty gallons or more. Jesus said, "Fill the jars with water." So they filled them up to the brim. Then he said, "Now take some out, and carry it to the manager of the feast." This they did, and when the manager of the feast tasted the water which had become wine, not knowing where it had come from, he called the bridegroom and said to him, "Everyone serves the good wine first, and then the poorer wine after the people have drunk freely, but you have kept the good wine until now."

This, the first of his signs, Jesus performed at Cana in Galilee, and thus showed forth his glory; and His disciples believed in Him.

JESUS CLEANSES THE TEMPLE

After the wedding at Cana Jesus and his disciples, together with his mother and brothers, went down to Capernaum, a town on the Sea of Galilee. Here Jesus later made his home, but this time he stayed only a few days, perhaps away from the crowd that had grown excited over his miracle in Cana. It was soon time for celebrating the passover of the Jews, so Jesus and His disciples made a journey to Jerusalem, where the great temple was located. During this stay in the Jewish capital Jesus did a startling thing that again showed that he was about his Father's business.

In the temple he found a noisy group of people buying and selling animals for sacrifice, and changing foreign money into Jewish coin so that travelers from afar could pay their temple tax in Jewish money. This market place had been established for the convenience of pilgrims who had long distances to travel. But the trouble with it was that it was located in the outer temple court, where men ought to have a chance to meditate and pray in quiet. After all, the temple was a place specially set aside for worship, and business could just as well be transacted elsewhere. Then, too, the arrangement became a means for the priests of the temple to charge high prices and reap large profits. So the profiteering of the priests and the commotion caused by the crowd, especially by the traders who were noisily selling their wares, created an atmosphere in the temple that was anything but reverent.

Then Jesus made a whip of small cords and drove them all out of the temple, with the sheep and oxen, and scattered the money-changers' coins upon the floor and overthrew their tables. "Take these things away," he said. "It is written, My house shall be a house of prayer, but you have made it a den of robbers!"

Then the Jews said to him, "What sign of authority have you to show us, seeing you do these things?" Jesus answered, "Destroy this temple, and in three days I will raise it up." But he spoke about the holy building which was his body. Later, when he had risen from the dead, his disciples remembered that he had said this, and they believed the word which Jesus had spoken.

THE CALLING OF MATTHEW

Later, when Jesus was back in Galilee, he passed by a tax-office. This was in charge of a man named Levi, but who later was called Matthew. The tax-office was probably located at Capernaum. If so, it was a very busy place, since the caravan road between Egypt and Damascus passed through the city.

When Jesus saw Matthew sitting at the place where taxes were collected, he said to him, "Follow me."

And he arose, and followed him, later being chosen as one of the twelve apostles.

In celebration of the great change that came into his life when he became a follower of Jesus, Matthew invited many of his friends to a feast in his home. Among these were other publicans (tax-collectors) and sinners (outcasts, especially those whom the Pharisees had excommunicated from the synagogue). When some of the Pharisees saw this, they said to his disciples, "Why does your Master eat with publicans and sinners?"

When Jesus heard it, he said, "They that are well do not need a physician, but those that are sick. Go and learn the meaning of this word, *I care for mercy, not for sacrifice.* For I have not come to call the righteous, but sinners to repentance."

119

Jesus said to Matthew, "Follow me"

120

CHAPTER FOUR

MIGHTY DEEDS OF JESUS

GALILEE

After a rather brief ministry in Jerusalem, our Lord returned to Galilee. Here he found the people much more friendly toward him than in Judea, which was the stronghold of the proud scribes and Pharisees.

A large part of the population in Galilee was made up of devout Jews who had a good religious background and yet were not as prejudiced and self-satisfied as the people of Judea. Galilee was a flourishing country, rich in resources, and thickly populated. According to Josephus, the great historian of the Jewish people, Galilee had 204 towns and cities. It was therefore a promising field for our Lord's ministry. Capernaum, a thriving city on the northwest shore of the Sea of Galilee, became his headquarters, and Jesus came to look upon it as his own city.

THE NOBLEMAN'S SON

Jesus came again to Cana of Galilee, where he made the water wine. And there was a certain nobleman, whose son was sick at Capernaum. When he heard that Jesus had come back to Galilee, he went to him, and begged him to come and heal his son who was at the point of death.

Jesus said to him, "Unless you see signs and wonders, you will not believe." The nobleman said to him, "Sir, come down before my child dies." Jesus said to him, "Go; your son will live." The man believed the word that Jesus spoke, and he went his way.

As he was going home, his servants met him and told him that his son lived. He inquired of them the hour when he began to get better. They told him, "Yesterday at the seventh hour the fever left him." So the father knew that it was at the very time when Jesus said to him, "Your son will live." And the nobleman believed, and his whole household.

THE GREAT CATCH OF FISHES

Jesus came to Galilee, to the city of Capernaum. And he went about all Galilee, teaching in their synagogues, and preaching the gospel of the king dom, and healing all manner of sickness among the people.

As the people crowded to be near him so as to hear the word of God, he was standing by the Sea of Galilee. Jesus saw two boats by the edge of the water, but the fishermen had gone out of them and were washing their nets. He got into one of the boats, belonging to Simon, and asked him to shove off a little way from the land. Then he sat down and taught the people on shore from the boat.

When he had finished speaking he said to Simon, "Put out into the deep, and let down your nets for a catch." Simon answered, "Master, we have toiled all the night, and have taken nothing; nevertheless at thy word I will let down the net." When they had done this, they got such a great number of fish, that their net began to break. And they signaled to their partners in the other boat to come and help them. They came and filled the two boats, so that they began to sink.

When Simon Peter saw this he fell down at the feet of Jesus, and said, "Depart from me, O Lord, for I am a sinner." For he was astonished, and all that were with him, at the number of fish which they had caught. And so were also James and John, the sons of Zebedee, who were partners with Simon. Then Jesus said to Simon, "Fear not, from now on you shall catch men." And when they had brought their boats to land, they left everything and followed him.

*"They filled
the two boats"*

122

The Sea of Galilee

A DAY OF HEALING IN CAPERNAUM

And they went to Capernaum; and on the sabbath day he entered into the synagogue and taught. The people were astonished at his teaching; for he taught them as one who had authority, and not as the scribes.

When they had come out of the synagogue, they went to the house of Simon Peter and Andrew, with James and John. Now Simon Peter's wife's mother lay sick with a fever, and they told Jesus of her. And he came and took her by the hand, and raised her up. The fever left her and she began to wait on them.

In the evening, when the sun had set, they brought to him all that were sick or possessed with demons. And the whole city was gathered together about the door. And he healed many that were sick with various diseases, and cast out many demons.

THE LEPER CLEANSED

And a leper came to him, and kneeling down before him, he said, "If thou wilt, thou canst make me clean." And being moved with pity, Jesus stretched out his hand and touched him, and said to him, "I will; be made clean."

And immediately the leprosy left him, and he was made clean. Then Jesus said to him, "See that you say nothing to any one: but go, show yourself to the priest, and offer for your cleansing what Moses commanded for a proof to the people." But the man went out and began to tell everyone and to spread the news in all directions, so that it was no longer possible

123

"He healed many that were sick"

124

for Jesus to go openly into any town, but he remained outside in desert places, and people came to him from every direction.

THE CENTURION'S SERVANT

A Roman centurion (captain) had a servant of whom he was very fond. This servant was sick and at the point of death. When the centurion heard about Jesus, he sent some elders of the Jews to him, to ask him to come and save his servant's life. And they went to Jesus and begged him to do it. "He deserves to have this done for him," they said, "for he loves the people of our nation, and it was he who built us our synagogue."

So Jesus went with them. When he was not far from the house, the centurion sent friends to him, to tell him, "Master, I am not good enough for you to come under my roof; that is why I did not think I was fit to come to you. But simply say the word, and my servant shall be made well. For I am myself a man under authority, having soldiers under me; and I say to this one, Go, and he goes; and to another, Come, and he comes; and to my servant, Do this, and he does it."

When Jesus heard this he was surprised, and said to the people who were with him, "Truly I tell you that I have not seen such great faith as this, no not in Israel. And I say to you that many shall come from the east and the west, and take their seats with Abraham, and Isaac, and Jacob, in the kingdom of heaven; but the sons of the kingdom shall be cast out into the outer darkness, and there shall be weeping and gnashing of teeth."

And when the messengers went back to the house, they found that the servant was well again.

THE BEJECTION AT NAZARETH

And he came to Nazareth, where he had been brought up: and on the sabbath he went to the synagogue, as was his custom, and stood up to read the Scriptures. And the book of the prophet Isaiah was handed to him. And he opened the book, and found the place where it was written,

> The Spirit of the Lord is upon me,
> Because he anointed me to preach good tidings to the poor:
> He hath sent me to proclaim release to the captives,
> And recovering of sight to the blind,
> To set at liberty them that are bruised,
> To proclaim the acceptable year of the Lord.

And he closed the book, and gave it back to the attendant, and sat down: and the eyes of all in the synagogue were fixed upon him. And he began by saying to them, "Today hath this scripture been fulfilled in your hearing." And all spoke well of him, and wondered at the words of grace which proceeded out of his mouth: and they said, "Is not this Joseph's son?" And he said to them, "Doubtless ye will say unto me this parable, Physician, heal thyself: whatsoever we have heard done at Capernaum, do also here in thine own country."

And he said, "Verily, I say unto you, No prophet is acceptable in his own country. But I tell you, there were many widows in Israel in the days of Elijah, when the heavens were closed three years and six months, when there came a great famine over all the land; and to none of them was Elijah sent, but only to Zarephath, in the land of Sidon, to a woman that was a widow. And there were many lepers in Israel in the time of Elisha the prophet; and none of them was cleansed, but only Naaman the Syrian."

And when the people in the synagogue heard these things, they were very angry; and they rose up, and drove him out of the city, and led him unto the brow of the hill on which their city was built, intending to cast him down headlong. But he passing through their midst went his way.

"The eyes of all in the synagogue were fixed upon him"

126

THE FEEDING OF THE FIVE THOUSAND

One day Jesus and his disciples sought rest by crossing over the Sea of Galilee to a desert place. But many people noticing the direction in which the boats went, made their way by land around the northern end of the lake and found Jesus not far from the place where the Jordan flows into it.

When Jesus saw how eager the people were, he had pity on them, so that he healed those of them who were ill and taught them many things.

The day wore on, but the people made no move to go. Finally the disciples asked Jesus to send them away, so that they might go and buy themselves some food. But Jesus said, "There is no need for them to go away: give them food yourselves." Philip answered, "Two hundred pennyworth (about thirty-five dollars) of bread would not be enough even to give every one a little."

Then Andrew, the brother of Simon Peter, said, "There is a lad here with five barley loaves and two small fishes; but what is that among so many people?"

Jesus said, "Let the people sit down." Now there was much grass in that place. And those seated on the grass were about five thousand.

Then Jesus took the bread and when he had given thanks, he gave it to the disciples, and the disciples to the people who were seated, and the fishes in the same way, as much as they needed. And when they had eaten their fill, he said to his disciples, "Gather up what is left over, so that nothing be lost." So they gathered up what was left over, and it filled twelve baskets.

And when the people saw the miracle which Jesus had performed, they said, "Truly this is the prophet who is to come into the world." And they were ready to come and take him by force to make him a king, but Jesus answered, "You came after me, not because you saw signs, but because you ate of the bread and were filled. Let your work not be for the bread that comes to an end, but for the food which endures to eternal life, which the Son of man shall give you. . . . I am the bread of life. He who comes to me shall never hunger and he who believes on me shall never thirst."

After that many of his disciples went back and would no longer follow him. So Jesus said to the twelve, "Will you also go away?" Simon Peter answered him, "Lord, to whom shall we go? Thou hast the words of eternal life."

JESUS STILLS THE STORM

The same day, when evening had come, Jesus went into a boat with his disciples to go over to the other side of the lake. But as they sailed, he fell asleep and a storm of wind came down on the lake. The boat was filling with water, and they were in great danger.

And they woke him, saying, "Master, Master, we perish!" Then he rose up and rebuked the wind and the raging of the water, saying, "Peace, be still!" And the wind stopped, and there was a great calm. And he said to them, "Why are you so fearful? Why have you no faith?"

Great fear came upon them, and they said one to another, "What manner of man is this, that even the wind and the waves obey him?"

THE WIDOW'S SON AT NAIN

One day Jesus went to a town called Nain; and his disciples went with him, and a great number of people. Now when he came near to the gate of the town, a dead man was being carried out, the only son of his mother, and she was a widow; and a great number of people of the town were with her.

When the Lord saw her, he had pity on her. "Do not weep," he said. He went up and touched the bier: and the bearers stopped. And he said, "Young man, I say to you, Arise." And he that was dead sat up, and began to speak. And Jesus gave him back to his mother.

And fear came on all: and they praised God, saying, "A great prophet is among us, and God has visited his people."

THE GREEK WOMAN'S DAUGHTER

One day Jesus went across the northern border of Galilee into the neighborhood of Tyre and Sidon. And he went into a certain house, and wanted no one to know it. But he could not keep it secret. Immediately a woman whose daughter had an unclean spirit came and threw herself at his feet. Now the woman was a Greek, of Syrophoenician birth. And she begged him to drive the demon out of her daughter.

He answered, "Let the children first eat all they want, for it is not right to take the children's bread and throw it to the dogs."

But she answered, "True, my Lord; and still the dogs under the table eat of the children's crumbs."

Jesus said to her, "O woman, great is your faith! Be it done for you as you desire. For those words of yours, go home." And her daughter was healed instantly.

A BLIND MAN RECEIVES SIGHT

They came to Jericho, and as Jesus was leaving that town with his disciples and a great crowd following him, Bartimaeus, a blind beggar, was sitting by the wayside. Hearing that Jesus of Nazareth was passing by, he began to cry out,

"Jesus, son of David, have mercy on me."

Many rebuked him for his shouting, but he only cried out the louder,

"Son of David, have mercy on me."

Then Jesus stood still. "Call him," he said.

So they called the blind man, and he came to Jesus.

"What do you want me to do for you?" asked Jesus.

"Lord," replied the blind man, "that I may receive my sight."

And Jesus answered, "Go. Your faith has made you well."

Immediately he received his sight, and followed Jesus along the road.

MARY AND MARTHA

One day Jesus entered into a certain village, and a certain woman named Martha received him into her house. And she had a sister called Mary, who also sat at Jesus' feet, and listened to his word. But Martha was worried about much serving, and came to him, and said, "Lord, dost thou not care that my sister hath left me to serve alone? Bid her therefore that she help me." And Jesus answered her, "Martha, Martha, thou art full of care and troubled about many things: but one thing is needful; Mary hath chosen that good part, which shall not be taken away from her."

JESUS BLESSING THE LITTLE CHILDREN

And they were bringing little children to him, to have him touch them: and the disciples rebuked them for it.

But when Jesus saw it, he was indignant, and said, "Suffer the little children to come unto me; forbid them not: for to such belongeth the kingdom of God. Verily I say unto you, Whosoever shall not receive the kingdom of God as a little child, he shall in no wise enter therein."

And he took them in his arms, and blessed them, laying his hands upon them.

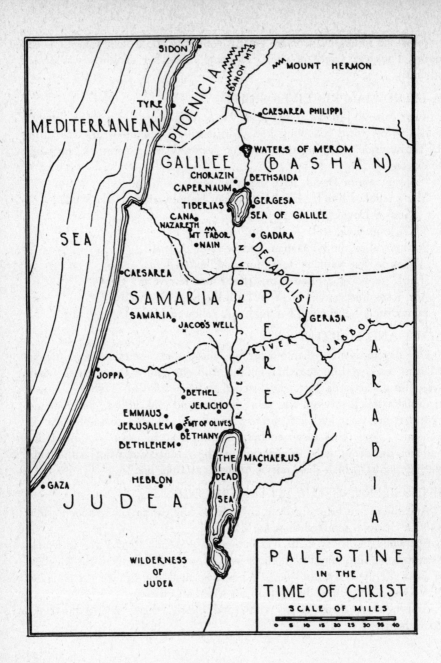

PALESTINE
IN THE
TIME OF CHRIST
SCALE OF MILES

CHAPTER FIVE

JESUS SENDS HIS DISCIPLES ON A MISSION

THE TWELVE

Jesus went up into a mountain to pray, and continued all night in prayer to God. When day came, he called his disciples to him, and he chose twelve of them, to whom he gave the name of apostles (i.e., messengers).

These are the names of the twelve apostles:

1) Simon, whom he also called Peter, and 2) Andrew his brother;

3) James, the son of Zebedee, and 4) John, his brother, whom he also surnamed Boanerges, meaning the sons of thunder;

5) Philip and 6) Bartholomew (or Nathanael);

7) Thomas and 8) Matthew (or Levi), the publican;

9) James, the son of Alpheus, and 10) Judas Lebbeus or Thaddeus.

11) Simon called Zelotes, and 12) Judas Iscariot, who also was the traitor.

These twelve Jesus sent on a mission after giving the following instructions, "Go nowhere among the Gentiles, and enter no town of the Samaritans: but go rather to the lost sheep of the house of Israel. And preach as you go, saying, The kingdom of heaven is at hand. Heal the sick, raise the dead, cleanse the lepers, cast out demons. You received without pay; give without pay. Take no gold, nor silver, nor copper in your purses; no bag for your journey, neither two coats, nor sandals, nor a staff: for the laborer deserves his food. And into whatever city or village you enter, find out who is worthy in it; and stay with him until you depart. As you enter the house, salute it. And if the house is worthy, let your peace come upon it; but if it be not worthy, let your peace return to you. And if any one will not receive you, or listen to your words, shake off the dust from your feet as you leave that house or town. Verily I say to you, It shall be more tolerable for the land of Sodom and Gomorrah in the day of Judgment than for that town."

Later the apostles came back and they told him all that they had done, and what they had taught. And he said to them, "Come away into a desert place, and rest a while." For there were so many coming and going that they could not find time to eat. And they went away in the boat to a desert place.

THE SEVENTY

Later in his ministry Jesus appointed seventy others and sent them on ahead of him, by twos, to go to every town or place where he himself was to come. And he said to them, "The harvest indeed is plentiful, but the laborers are few. Pray therefore the Lord of the harvest to send out laborers into his harvest. Now go your ways; I am sending you as lambs into the midst of wolves. Carry no purse, bag, nor change of shoes; and do not stop to salute any man on the road.

"Whatever house you enter, first say, 'Peace be to this house!' And if a son of peace is there, your peace shall rest upon him; but if not, it shall return to you. And remain in that same house, eating and drinking what they provide, for the laborer deserves his wages. Do not move from one house to another.

"And into whatever city you enter and they receive you, eat what they set before you. Heal the sick in that town and tell them that the kingdom of God has come to them. But whatever city you enter into and they do not receive you, go out into the streets and say, 'Even the dust of your town that clings to our feet we wipe off as a protest; nevertheless know this, that the kingdom of God has come near.'

"He who listens to you listens to me, and he who rejects you rejects me, and he who rejects me rejects him who sent me."

Later the seventy returned with joy. "Even the demons obey us," they said. And Jesus answered, "I saw Satan fall like a flash of lightning from heaven. Nevertheless, do not rejoice in this, that the evil spirits obey you, but rejoice that your names are written in heaven."

Bethany, the Town in Which Martha, Mary and Lazarus Lived

Wide World Photo

CHAPTER SIX

TEACHINGS OF JESUS

When Jesus spoke, the people were aware of a power and authority that the scribes and Pharisees did not possess. Somehow he was different. Being the Son of God he never needed to guess or speculate. He knew.

"You have heard that it was said of them of old, but I say unto you"— we hear words like these falling from his lips again and again. He was sure of both himself and his message.

But Christ never demanded that people believe him just because he said a thing. They could also see what he was doing. More than that, they could try his teaching out in daily life and find out for themselves how true it was. "My teaching is not mine, but his that sent me. If any man is willing to do his will, he shall come to know whether what I say is of God or of men."

God's work of making himself known was not completed in the Old Testament. This revelation was continued and fulfilled through the coming of Christ.

In our study so far we have already learned something of the teachings of Jesus. The events that are recorded tell us much. However, there are in the four gospels of the New Testament a number of sermons or discourses and parables that tell us still more. The purpose of this chapter is to study these important sayings of our Lord.

THE SERMON ON THE MOUNT

After choosing the Twelve, Jesus preached what has come to be known as the Sermon on the Mount. It is so called because he was on a mountain, perhaps one of the high hills near the southwestern shore of the Sea of Galilee, when he spoke these famous words. They make up the longest address of Jesus recorded in the Scriptures.

The Beatitudes

Blessed are the poor in spirit, for theirs is the kingdom of heaven.

Blessed are they that mourn, for they shall be comforted.

Blessed are the meek, for they shall inherit the earth.

Blessed are they that hunger and thirst after righteousness, for they shall be filled.

Blessed are the merciful, for they shall obtain mercy.

Blessed are the pure in heart, for they shall see God.

Blessed are the peacemakers, for they shall be called the sons of God.

Blessed are they that have been persecuted for righteousness' sake, for theirs is the kingdom of heaven. Blessed are you when men shall revile you and persecute you and say all manner of evil against you falsely, for my sake. Rejoice and be glad, for great is your reward in heaven: for so persecuted they the prophets that were before you.

The Law

Think not that I have come to abolish the law and prophets; I have come not to abolish them but to fulfill them. For truly I say to you, till heaven and earth pass away, not one iota, not a dot, shall pass from the law till all is fulfilled. For I say to you, unless your righteousness exceeds the righteousness of the scribes and Pharisees, you will never enter into the kingdom of heaven.

Love to Our Neighbor

You have heard that it was said, You shall love your neighbor and hate your enemy; but I say unto you, Love your enemies, do good to those who hate you, bless those who curse you, and pray for those who abuse you, that you may be the sons of your Father who is in heaven; for he makes his sun to rise on the evil and on the good, and sends rain on the just and on the unjust. You, therefore, must be perfect, as your heavenly father is perfect.

The Chief Care in This Life

Do not lay up for yourselves treasures on earth, where moth and rust consume and where thieves break in and steal, but lay up for yourselves treasures in heaven, where neither moth nor rust consumes and where thieves do not break in and steal; for where your treasure is, there will your heart be also. Do not be anxious about your life, what you shall eat or what you shall drink, nor about your body, what you shall put on. Is not life more than food, and the body than clothing? Look at the birds of the air: they neither sow nor reap nor gather into barns, and yet your heavenly Father feeds them. Are you not much more than they? Which of you by taking thought, can add to the span of his life? And why be anxious about clothing? Consider the lilies of the field, how they grow; they toil not, neither do they spin. And yet I say to you, that even Solomon in all his glory was not arrayed like one of these. Therefore, do not be anxious, saying, What shall we eat, or what shall we drink, or wherewithal shall we be clothed? For after all these things do the Gentiles seek. But seek first the kingdom of God and his righteousness, and all these things shall be yours as well.

Uncharitable Judgment Forbidden

Judge not, that you be not judged. For with the judgment you pronounce, you shall be judged: and the measure you give, shall be the measure you get. Why do you see the speck that is in your brother's eye, but do not see the log that is in your own eye? Or how can you say to your brother, Let me take the speck out of your eye, when there is a log in your own eye? You hypocrite, first take the log out of your own eye, and then you will see clearly to take the speck out of your brother's eye.

The Right Way

Enter by the narrow gate: for wide is the gate, and easy is the way, that leads to destruction, and those who enter by it are many. For narrow is the gate, and hard is the way, that leads to life, and those who find it are few.

Building on the Rock

Not every one who says to me, "Lord, Lord," shall enter the kingdom of heaven; but he who does the will of my Father who is in heaven. On that day many will say to me, "Lord, Lord, did we not prophesy in your name, and cast out demons in your name, and do many mighty works in your name?" And then I will declare to them, "I never knew you; depart from me, you evil-doers."

Every one then who hears these words of mine and does them will be like a wise man who built his house upon the rock: and the rain fell and the floods came, and the winds blew and beat upon that house, but it did not fall, because it had been founded upon the rock. And every one who hears these words of mine and does not do them will be a foolish man who built his house upon the sand; and the rain fell, and the floods came, and the winds blew and beat against that house, and it fell: and great was the fall of it.

PARABLES OF THE KINGDOM OF GOD

A parable is a short story that carries a moral or spiritual lesson. Jesus often used parables in his teaching, and they served two very good purposes: they attracted the attention of the listeners, and they helped the listeners understand the truth that he was teaching. The parables of Jesus are always interesting and they make plain many truths that we need to know and live by today.

The Sower

Jesus said, "Listen! A sower went out to sow. And as he sowed, some seed fell along the path, and the birds came and devoured it. Other seed fell on rocky ground, where it had not much soil, and immediately it sprang up, since it had no depth of soil; and when the sun rose it was scorched, and since it had no root it withered away. Other seed fell among thorns and the thorns grew up and choked it, and it yielded no grain. And other seed fell into good soil and brought forth grain, growing up and increasing and yielding thirtyfold and sixtyfold and hundredfold." And he said, "He who has ears to hear, let him hear."

And his disciples asked him, "What does this parable mean?" And he said, "The seed is the word of God. Those by the way-side are they that hear; then comes the devil, and takes away the word out of their hearts, lest they should believe and be saved. Those on the rock are people who, when they hear, receive the word with joy; but they have no root; for a time they believe, but in time of temptation they fall away. That which fell among thorns means those who, when they have heard, go on their way and are choked with cares and riches and pleasures of this life, and bring no fruit to perfection. But that on the good ground means those who, having listened to the word with open minds and a right spirit, keep it, and bring forth fruit with patience."

The Tares

"The kingdom of heaven is like a man who sowed good seed in his field. but during the night his enemy came and sowed tares among the wheat, and went his way. When the blade had sprung up, and the grain was formed, then appeared the tares also. So the farmer's men came and said to him, "Sir, was it not good seed that you sowed in your field? Where then do the tares come from?" "An enemy has done this," he said. The men said, "Shall we go and gather them up?" But he answered, "No, lest while you gather up the tares you should at the same time root up the wheat with them. Let both grow together until the harvest; and at the time of harvest I will tell the reapers to gather together first the tares, and bind them in bundles to burn; but to bring all the wheat into my barn."

"Unless your righteousness exceeds the righteousness of the scribes and Pharisees, you will never enter into the kingdom of heaven"

COPR. BY PROVIDENCE LITHOGRAPH CO.

137

When his disciples asked him to explain this parable, he answered, "The sower of the good seed is the Son of man; the field is the world; the good seed — these are the children of the kingdom; but the tares are the children of the evil one. The enemy who sowed the tares is the devil; the harvest is the end of the world; and the reapers are the angels. As therefore the tares are gathered and burned in the fire, so shall it be in the end of this world. The Son of man shall send forth his angels, and they shall gather out of his kingdom all things that cause sin, and all who break his laws, and these they shall cast into a furnace of fire: there shall be wailing and gnashing of teeth. Then shall the righteous shine as the sun in the kingdom of their Father."

The Mustard Seed

Jesus said, "The kingdom of heaven is like a grain of mustard seed, which a man took and sowed in his field: which indeed is the least of all seeds; but when it is grown, it is the greatest among herbs, and becomes a tree, so that the birds of the air come and lodge in the branches of it."

The Leaven

Jesus said, "The kingdom of heaven is like leaven, which a woman took, and hid in three measures of meal, till the whole was leavened."

The Hidden Treasure

Jesus said, "Again, the kingdom of heaven is like treasure hidden in a field, which a man found and covered up; then in his joy he goes and sells all that he has and buys that field."

The Pearl of Great Price

Jesus said, "Again, the kingdom of heaven is like a merchant in search of fine pearls; who, when he had found one pearl of great value, went out and sold all that he had and bought it."

The Net

Jesus said, "Again, the kingdom of heaven is like a net which was cast into the sea and gathered fish of every kind; when it was full, men drew it to shore, and sat down and sorted the good into vessels but threw the bad away. So shall it be at the end of the world: the angels shall come forth and separate the wicked from the righteous, and shall throw them into the furnace of fire: there shall be wailing and gnashing of teeth."

The Ten Virgins

The kingdom of heaven is like ten virgins, who took their lamps, and went forth to meet the bridegroom. And five of them were foolish, and five were wise. For the foolish, when they took their lamps, took no oil with them: but the wise took oil in their vessels with their lamps.

Now while the bridegroom was delayed, they all slumbered and slept. But at midnight there was a cry, "Behold, the bridegroom! Come to meet him."

Then all those virgins arose, and trimmed their lamps. And the foolish said to the wise, "Give us some of your oil; for our lamps are going out." But the wise answered, "Perhaps there will not be enough for us and you: go rather to those who sell, and buy for yourselves."

And while they went away to buy, the bridegroom came; and those who were ready went in with him to the marriage feast: and the door was shut. Afterward came also the other virgins, saying, "Lord, Lord, open to us." But he answered and said, "Verily I say to you, I know you not." Watch therefore, for you know neither the day nor the hour.

The Prodigal Son

Now all the publicans and sinners came near to Jesus to hear him. And the Pharisees and scribes found fault, saying, "This man receives sinners and eats with them." Then Jesus told them this parable:

A certain man had two sons; and the younger of them said to his father, "Father, give me the part of your property which will be mine." And the father divided his property between them. And not many days after, the younger gathered together all that he had and journeyed into a far country. There he wasted his money in loose living.

And when he had spent all, there arose a great famine in that country; and he began to be in want. And he went and hired out to a citizen of that country; and he sent him into his fields to feed swine. So great was his hunger that he would have been glad to eat the pigs' food, but no one gave him anything.

And when he came to himself, he said, "How many hired servants of my father's have bread enough and to spare, and I am dying of hunger! I will arise and go to my father, and will say to him, 'Father, I have sinned against heaven, and before you, and am no more worthy to be called your son: make me as one of your hired servants.' "

And he arose, and went to his father. But when he was still far away, his father saw him, and was moved with pity for him, and ran, and took him in his arms, and kissed him. And the son said to him, "Father, I have sinned against heaven and before you, and am no more worthy to be called your son." But the father said to his servants, "Bring quickly the best robe, and put it on him; and put a ring on his hand, and shoes on his feet; and bring the fatted calf, and kill it; and let us eat and be merry: for this my son was dead, and is alive again; he was lost, and is found." And they began to be merry.

Now the elder son was in the field; and as he came near the house, he heard music and dancing. And he called one of the servants and asked what this meant. And he said to him, "Your brother has come; and your father has killed the fatted calf, because he has received him safe and sound." And the brother was angry, and would not go in: therefore his father came out and urged him to come in. But he said to his father, "Lo, these many years I have served you, neither have I ever disobeyed your orders; and yet you never gave me even a young goat, that I might have a feast with my friends: but as soon as this son of yours came, who has been wasting your property with bad women, you have killed for him the fatted calf!" And he said to him, "Son, you are always with me, and all that I have is yours. It was right that we should make merry and be glad; for this your brother was dead, and is alive again; and was lost, and is found."

The Unmerciful Servant

Peter came to Jesus one day and said, "Lord, how often shall my brother sin against me, and I forgive him? Till seven times?" Jesus said to him, "I say not, Until seven times; but, Until seventy times seven."

"The kingdom of heaven is like a certain king, who went over his accounts with his servants. And when he had begun to reckon, a servant was brought to him, who owed him ten thousand talents (about $10,000,000 in our money). And because he could not pay it, his lord commanded him to be sold, and his wife, and children and all that he had, and payment to be made. The servant therefore fell down, and did homage to him, saying, "Lord, have patience with me, and I will pay you all!" Then the lord forgave him the debt.

140

The same servant went out, and found one of his fellow servants, who owed him a hundred pence (about $17.50), and he laid hands on him, and took him by the throat, saying, "Pay me what you owe." And his fellow servant fell down at his feet, and begged him, saying, "Have patience with me and I will pay you all." And he would not; but went and put him in prison, till he should pay the debt.

When his fellow servants saw what was done, they were very sorry, and came and told their lord of what was done. Then his lord, after he had called him, said to him, "You wicked servant! I forgave you all that debt, because you asked me: should you not also have had mercy on your fellow servant, even as I had pity on you?" Then his lord was angry, and put him in the hands of those who would punish him, till he made payment of all the debt.

So likewise shall my heavenly Father do also to you, if you do not from your hearts every one give forgiveness to his brother.

The Great Supper

One day Jesus went to dinner at the home of an important Pharisee. And one of those who sat at the table said, "Blessed is he that shall eat bread in the kingdom of God." Then Jesus told a parable:

A certain man made a great supper, and invited many; when the time had come he sent his servants to say to them, "Come, for all things are now ready." And they all began to offer excuses for not coming. The first said, "I have bought a piece of ground, I must go and see it: I beg you to have me excused." And another said, "I have bought five yoke of oxen, and I go to try them: I beg you to have me excused." And another said, "I have married a wife: and therefore I cannot come." So the servant came back and gave his master an account of these things.

Then the master of the house was angry and said to his servant, "Go out quickly into the streets and lanes of the city, and bring in the poor, and the maimed, and the blind and the lame." And the servant said, "Lord, it is done as thou hast commanded, and still there is room." And the Lord said to the servant, "Go out into the highways and fields, and compel them to come in, that my house may be filled. For I say to you, that none of those men who were invited shall taste of my supper."

The Use of Talents

A nobleman went into a far country to receive kingly power and then return. Calling ten of his servants, he gave them ten pounds, and said to them, "Trade with these till I come."

When he returned, having received the kingly power, he commanded these servants, to whom he had given the money, to be called to him, that he might know what they gained by trading. The first came before him, saying, "Lord, your pound has made ten pounds more." And he said to him, "Well done, good servant! Because you have been faithful in a very little, you shall have authority over ten cities." And the second came, saying, "Lord, your pound has made five pounds." And he said to him, "And you are to be over five cities." Then another came, saying, "Lord, here is your pound, which I kept laid away in a napkin; for I was afraid of you, because you are a severe man; you take up what you did not lay down, and reap what you did not sow."

He said to him, "I will condemn you out of your own mouth, you wicked servant! You knew that I was a severe man, taking up what I did not lay down and reaping what I did not sow? Why then did you not put my money into the bank, and at my coming I should have collected it with interest?" And he said to those who stood by, "Take the pound from him, and give it to him who has the ten pounds." "I tell you, that to every one who has will more be given; but from him who has not, even what he has will be taken away."

COPR. BY PROVIDENCE LITHOGRAPH CO.

"To everyone who has will more be given"

142

THE HEAVENLY FATHER AND HIS CHILDREN

Prayer

One of his disciples said to Jesus, "Lord, teach us to pray, as John also taught his disciples." And he said:

When ye pray, say: Our Father who art in heaven, Hallowed be thy name. Thy kingdom come. Thy will be done on earth as it is in heaven. Give us this day our daily bread. And forgive us our trespasses as we forgive those who trespass against us. And lead us not into temptation, but deliver us from evil: for thine is the kingdom, and the power, and the glory, for ever. Amen.

Ask, and it shall be given you; seek, and ye shall find; knock, and it shall be opened unto you. For every one that asketh receiveth; and he that seeketh, findeth, and to him that knocketh it shall be opened. Or what man is there of you, who if his son ask bread, will he give him a stone? Or, if he ask a fish, will he give him a serpent? If ye then, being evil, know how to give good gifts unto your children: how much more shall your heavenly Father give the Holy Spirit to them that ask him?

Faith

Jesus said to them: Have faith in God. Verily I say to you, Whosoever shall say to this mountain, Be thou taken up and cast into the sea, and shall not doubt in his heart, but shall believe that what he saith cometh to pass, he shall have it. Therefore I say to you, All things whatsoever ye pray and ask for, believe that ye receive them, and ye shall have them.

Obedience

Jesus said to them: My meat is to do the will of him that sent me, and to accomplish his work. . . . If any man willeth to do his will, he shall know of the teaching, whether it is of God, or whether I speak from myself. . . . Ye are my friends, if ye do the things which I command you.

Courage

And you shall be hated by all men for my name's sake; but he that endures to the end, the same shall be saved. And be not afraid of them that kill the body, but are not able to kill the soul: but rather fear him who is able to destroy both soul and body in hell. Are not two sparrows sold for a penny? and not one of them shall fall on the ground without your Father: but the very hairs of your head are all numbered. Fear not therefore: you are of more value than many sparrows. Every one therefore who shall confess me before men, him will I also confess before my Father who is in heaven. But whosoever shall deny me before men, him will I also deny before my Father who is in heaven.

Faithfulness

Let your loins be girded and your lamps burning; and be like men looking for their master to come home from the marriage feast, so that they may open to him at once when he comes and knocks. Blessed are those servants whom the master finds watching when he comes; verily I say to you, he will gird himself and have them sit at table and come and serve them. And if he comes in the second watch, or in the third, and finds them so, blessed are those servants! But know this, that if the master of the house had known at what hour the thief was coming, he would have watched, and not have left his house to be broken into. You must also be ready: for the Son of man is coming at an hour you do not expect.

"He who is faithful in a very little is faithful also in much; and he who is dishonest in a very little is dishonest also in much. If then you have not been faithful in the unrighteous mammon, who will entrust to you the true riches? And if you have not been faithful in that which is another's, who will give you that which is your own? No servant can serve two masters; for either he will hate the one and love the other, or he will be devoted to the one and despise the other. You cannot serve God and mammon."

Love

If a man loves me, he will keep my word, and my Father will love him, and we will come to him and make our home with him. He who does not love me does not keep my words; and the word which you hear is not mine but the Father's who sent me.

This is my commandment, that you love one another as I have loved you. Greater love has no man than this, that a man lay down his life for his friends.

And one of the scribes came up and heard them disputing with one another, and seeing that he answered them well, asked him, "Which commandment

144

is the first of all?" Jesus answered, "The first is, 'Hear, O Israel: The Lord our God, the Lord is one; and you shall love the Lord your God with all your heart, and with all your soul, and with all your mind, and with all your strength.' The second is this, 'You shall love your neighbor as yourself.' There is no other commandment greater than these." And the scribe said to him, "You are right, Teacher; you have truly said that he is one, and there is no other but he; and to love him with all the heart, and with all the understanding, and with all the strength, and to love one's neighbor as oneself, is much more than all whole burnt offerings and sacrifices." And when Jesus saw that he answered wisely, he said to him, "You are not far from the kingdom of God." And after that no one dared to ask him any question.

Generosity

Take heed, and keep yourselves from all covetousness: for a man's life consists not in the abundance of the things which he possesses.

And he told them a parable, saying, "The land of a rich man brought forth plentifully; and he thought to himself, 'What shall I do, for I have nowhere to store my crops?' And he said, 'I will do this: I will pull down my barns, and build larger ones; and there I will store all my grain and my goods. And I will say to my soul, Soul, you have ample goods laid up for many years; take your ease, eat, drink, be merry.' But God said to him, 'Fool! This night your soul is required of you; and the things you have prepared, whose will they be?' So is he who lays up treasures for himself, and is not rich toward God.

And he sat down opposite the treasury, and watched the multitude putting money into the treasury. Many rich people put in large sums. And a poor widow came, and put in two copper coins, which make a penny. And he called his disciples to him, and said to them, "Truly, I say to you, this poor widow has put in more than all those who are contributing to the treasury. For they all contributed out of their abundance; but she out of her poverty has put in everything she had, her whole living."

Rest for Your Souls

Come unto me, all ye that labor and are heavy laden, and I will give you rest. Take my yoke upon you, and learn of me; for I am meek and lowly in heart: and ye shall find rest unto your souls. For my yoke is easy, and my burden is light.

THE CHRISTIAN LIFE

The New Birth

There was a man of the Pharisees, named Nicodemus, a ruler of the Jews, who came to Jesus by night and said to him, "Rabbi, we know that thou art a teacher come from God; for no man can do these miracles that thou doest, except God be with him." Jesus answered, "Verily, verily, I say unto thee: Except a man be born again, he cannot see the kingdom of God."

Nicodemus said to him, "How can a man be born when he is old? Is it possible for him to enter a second time into his mother's body and be born again?" Jesus answered, "Verily, verily, I say unto thee: Except a man be born of water and of the Spirit, he cannot enter into the kingdom of God. That which is born of the flesh is flesh, and that which is born of the Spirit is spirit."

Nicodemus said to him, "How can these things be?" Jesus answered, "Art thou a teacher of Israel and knowest not these things? As Moses lifted up the serpent in the wilderness, even so must the Son of man be lifted up, that whosoever believeth in him should not perish, but have eternal life. For God so loved the world, that he gave his only begotten Son, that whosoever believeth in him should not perish, but have everlasting life. For God sent not his Son into the world to condemn the world, but that the world through him might be saved."

The Living Water

Jesus came to a city of Samaria named Sychar, near to the parcel of ground that Jacob gave to his son Joseph. And Jacob's well was there. Being weary from his journey, Jesus sat resting at the well. It was about noon.

Then came a woman of Samaria to draw water. Jesus said to her, "Give me to drink." The woman answered, "How is it that thou, being a Jew, askest drink of me, a woman of Samaria?" She said this because the Jews have no dealings with the Samaritans. Jesus answered, "If thou knewest the gift of God, and who it is that saith to thee: Give me to drink, thou wouldst have asked of him, and he would have given thee living water." The woman said, "Sir, thou hast nothing to draw with, and the well is deep: whence then hast thou that living water?" Jesus answered, "Whosoever drinketh of this water shall thirst again; but whosoever drinketh of the water that I shall give him shall never thirst." The woman said to him, "Sir, give me this water, that I thirst not, neither come hither to draw."

Jesus said to her, "Go, call thy husband and come hither." The woman answered, "I have no husband." Jesus said, "Thou hast spoken the truth, for thou hast had five husbands, and he whom thou now hast is not thy husband." The woman answered, "Sir, I perceive that thou art a prophet. Our fathers worshipped in this mountain (Gerizim), and ye say, that in Jerusalem is the place, where men ought to worship."

Jesus said to her, "The hour cometh, and now is, when the true worshippers shall worship the Father in Spirit and in truth. God is a Spirit, and they that worship him must worship him in Spirit and in truth." Then said the woman, "I know that the Messiah cometh, who is called Christ; when he hath come, he will tell us all things." Jesus said to her, "I that speak unto thee am he."

The woman then left her waterpot, and went into the city and said to the men, "Come, see a man who told me all things that ever I did: is not this the Christ?" Then they went out of the city, and came to him. And many of the Samaritans believed on him because of the saying of the woman. And they begged him to stay with them, and he was with them two days.

*Ruins of
Ancient
Samaritan
City*

*Underwood and
Underwood Photo*

And many more believed because of his own word, and they said, "We have heard him ourselves, and know that this is indeed the Christ, the Saviour of the world."

The Bread of Life

The next day after Jesus had fed five thousand people with five barley loaves and fishes, the crowd came to take him by force and make him their king. Such a man, they thought, would be just the kind of king they needed. But Jesus was not pleased with their plan. He had not come to set up a kingdom of this world, but to establish the kingdom of God. And the greatest need before the people was not, how shall we keep our bodies alive, but, how shall we keep our souls alive? So, when the crowd came to make him a king who could give them what they wanted for their physical life, our Lord spoke to them of their need of the spiritual food which he had come to give. This passage is called the Discourse on the Bread of Life:

Jesus answered them and said, "Verily, verily, I say unto you, Ye seek me, not because ye saw signs, but because ye ate of the loaves, and were filled. Work not for the food which perisheth, but for the food which abideth unto eternal life, which the Son of man shall give unto you: for him the Father, even God, hath sealed." They said therefore to him, "What must we do, that we may work the works of God?"

Jesus said to them, "This is the work of God, and ye believe on him whom he hath sent." They said therefore to him, "What then doest thou for a sign, that we may see, and believe thee? What workest thou? Our fathers ate the manna in the wilderness; as it is written, He gave them bread out of heaven to eat." Jesus therefore said to them, "Verily, verily, I say unto you, It was not Moses that gave you the bread out of heaven; but my Father giveth you the true bread out of heaven. For the bread of God is that which cometh down out of heaven, and giveth life unto the world." They said therefore unto him, "Lord, evermore give us this bread." Jesus said to them, "I am the bread of life: he that cometh to me shall not hunger, and he that believeth on me shall never thirst."

The Light of the World

Again therefore Jesus spoke to them, saying, "I am the light of the world: he that followeth me shall not walk in the darkness, but shall have the light of life."

The Good Shepherd

I am the good shepherd: the good shepherd layeth down his life for the sheep. He that is a hireling, and not a shepherd, whose own the sheep are not, beholdeth the wolf coming, and leaveth the sheep, and fleeth, and the wolf snatcheth them, and scattereth them: he fleeth because he is a hireling, and careth not for the sheep. I am the good shepherd; and I know mine own, and mine own know me, even as the Father knoweth me, and I know the Father; and I lay down my life for the sheep. And other sheep I have, which are not of this fold: them also I must bring and they shall hear my voice; and they shall become one flock, one shepherd. Therefore doth the Father love me, because I lay down my life, that I may take it again. No one taketh it away from me, but I lay it down of myself. I have power to lay it down, and I have power to take it again.

My sheep hear my voice, and I know them, and they follow me: and I give unto them eternal life; and they shall never perish, and no one shall snatch them out of my hand. My father, who hath given them unto me, is greater than all; and no one is able to snatch them out of the Father's hand.

A Shepherd and his Sheep Near Bethlehem

Wide World Photo

The True Vine

I am the true vine, and my Father is the husbandman. Every branch in me that beareth not fruit, he taketh it away: and every branch that beareth fruit, he cleanseth it, that it may bear more fruit. Already ye are clean because of the word which I have spoken unto you. Abide in me, and I in you. As the branch cannot bear fruit of itself, except it abide in the vine; so neither can ye, except ye abide in me.

I am the vine, ye are the branches: He that abideth in me, and I in Him, the same beareth much fruit: for apart from me ye can do nothing. If a man abide not in me, he is cast forth as a branch, and is withered; and they gather them, and cast them into the fire, and they are burned. If ye abide in me, and my words abide in you, ask whatsoever ye will, and it shall be done unto you. Herein is my Father glorified, that ye bear much fruit; and so shall ye be my disciples.

Hills of Northern Palestine

Associated Press Photo

CHAPTER SEVEN

JESUS AND JOHN THE BAPTIST

Soon after the wedding feast at Cana, Jesus went up to Jerusalem to attend the first Passover after beginning his public ministry. At Jerusalem he drove the traders out of the temple and held the conversation with Nicodemus concerning the new birth. He did not stay long in Jerusalem, however.

THE FRIEND OF THE BRIDEGROOM

After these things Jesus and his disciples went into the land of Judea; there he remained with them and baptized. John also was baptizing in Aenon near to Salim, because there was much water there: and people came and were baptized. For John had not yet been put in prison.

Now a discussion arose between John's disciples and a Jew about purifying. And they came to John, and said to him, "Rabbi, he who was with you beyond the Jordan, to whom you bore witness, here he is, baptizing, and all are going to him." John answered, "No man can receive anything except what is given him from heaven. You yourselves bear me witness, that I said, I am not the Christ, but I have been sent before him. He who has the bride is the bridegroom; the friend of the bridegroom, who stands and hears him, rejoices greatly at the bridegroom's voice; Therefore, this joy of mine is now full. He must increase, but I must decrease.

"He who comes from above is above all: he who is of the earth belongs to the earth, and of the earth he speaks: he that comes from heaven is above all."

ART THOU HE THAT IS TO COME?

When John heard in prison the works of Christ, he sent his disciples to ask him, "Art thou he that is to come, or shall we look for another?"

Jesus answered and said to them, "Go and tell John the things which you hear and see: the blind receive their sight, and the lame walk, the lepers are cleansed, and the deaf hear, and the dead are raised up, and the poor have good tidings preached to them. And blessed is he, whosoever shall find no occasion of stumbling in me."

As they went away, Jesus began to say to the crowds concerning John, "What did you go out into the wilderness to behold? A reed shaken with the wind? Why then did you go out? To see a man clothed in soft raiment? Behold, those who wear soft raiment are in kings' houses. Why then did you go out? To see a prophet? Yes, I tell you, and much more than a prophet. This is he of whom it is written,

> Behold, I send my messenger before thy face,
> Who shall prepare the way before thee.

"Verily I say to you, Among them that are born of women there has not risen a greater than John the Baptist: yet he who is least in the kingdom of heaven is greater than he."

THE DEATH OF JOHN THE BAPTIST

Herod had put John the Baptist in prison. The reason was that Herod had divorced his wife and married Herodias, the wife of his brother Philip, and John the Baptist had told him that this was wrong. Herod was very angry with John and would have put him to death, but he feared the crowd, because they looked upon John as a prophet.

When Herod's birthday came, the daughter of Herodias danced at the entertainment that was given. Her dancing pleased Herod so much that he promised with an oath to give her whatever she might ask. After consulting with her mother she came to Herod and said, "Give me the head of John the Baptist on a platter."

The king was sorry that he had made such a foolish promise, but he did not dare to break his oath. So he ordered his men to behead John in prison. And John's head was brought in on a platter to the daughter of Herodias, and she brought it to her mother.

John's disciples came and took the body and buried it; then they went and told Jesus. Later, when Herod heard of the mighty deeds of Jesus his conscience troubled him greatly and he said to his servants, "This is John the Baptist; he is risen from the dead; and therefore these powers work in him."

CHAPTER EIGHT

THE CONFLICT IN GALILEE

THE SCRIBES AND PHARISEES

The scribes and Pharisees were religious people who found much fault with Jesus. They considered themselves better than other folk because they felt that they kept religious rules much better than did the common people. They were proud and self-satisfied instead of humble before God. To them religion was more a matter of observing outward rules than a matter of love and honesty and humility. Jesus criticized them for this when, for example, he said:

"Well did Isaiah prophesy of you hypocrites, as it is written.

'This people honors me with their lips,
But their heart is far from me.
But in vain do they worship me,
Teaching as their doctrines the precepts of men'."

JESUS AND THE SABBATH

One Sabbath day Jesus and his disciples were going through a field of grain. As they walked, they pulled off some of the grain from the stalks and after rubbing it between their hands to get rid of the chaff, they began to eat the kernels. Some Pharisees saw it and found fault with Jesus and his disciples. Pulling off the heads of grain was the same as reaping, they thought, and rubbing away the chaff was the same as threshing. Both were forbidden on the Sabbath.

"Why do your disciples do what is not lawful?" they asked. But Jesus answered them, "The Sabbath was made for man, and not man for the Sabbath: so the Son of man is lord even of the Sabbath."

JESUS HEALS A MAN WITH A WITHERED HAND

Jesus went into a synagogue on the Sabbath and explained the Scriptures. A man was there whose right hand was withered, and the scribes and the Pharisees watched him to see if he would heal on the Sabbath day, so that they might find something against him.

153

"Arise, and take up your bed, and go home"

154

But Jesus knew their thoughts, and he said to the man with the withered hand, "Rise and come forward." And the man rose and came forward. Then he said to them, "Is it lawful on the Sabbath day to do good or to do evil, to save life, or to destroy it?" But they kept silence. When he had looked around at them he was angry, being grieved because of their hard hearts. Then he said to the man, "Hold out your hand." And he held it out, and his hand was made well like the other. The angry Pharisees went out and immediately began to plan how they might put him to death.

JESUS HEALS A MAN WHO WAS PARALYZED

One day, when Jesus was teaching in Capernaum, a man who was paralyzed was being carried to Jesus on a bed. The friends who carried him could not get him into the house on account of the crowd, so they went up on the roof and let him down on his bed through the tiles into the crowd in front of Jesus.

When Jesus saw their faith, he said to the sick man, "Son, your sins are forgiven." But there were some of the scribes who began to argue, saying, "Why does this man show such disrespect for God? Who can forgive sins but God only?" But immediately Jesus saw what they were discussing, and he said to them, "Which is easier to say: Your sins are forgiven, or to say: Arise, take up your bed and walk? But that you may know that the Son of man has power on earth to forgive sins:" —he said to the paralyzed man —"Arise, and take up your bed, and go home." And immediately he arose took up his bed and walked away praising God. They were all amazed, and praised God, saying, "We have seen strange things today."

THE PHARISEES DEMAND A SIGN FROM HEAVEN

And the Pharisees came, and began to question him, seeking from him a sign from heaven. And he sighed deeply and said, "Why does this generation seek for a sign? Verily I say to you, No sign shall be given to it but the sign of Jonah. For as Jonah became a sign to the men of Nineveh, so shall also the Son of man be to this generation. The queen of the South shall rise up at the judgment with the men of this generation and condemn them; for she came from the ends of the earth to hear the wisdom of Solomon; and behold, a greater than Solomon is here. The men of Nineveh shall arise at the judgment with this generation, and shall condemn it; for they repented at the preaching of Jonah; and behold, a greater than Jonah is here."

A Main Street in Bethlehem

CHAPTER NINE

THE SHADOW OF THE CROSS

PETER'S CONFESSION

When Jesus came into the area of Caesarea Philippi, he asked his disciples, "Who do men say that the Son of man is?" And they said, "Some say John the Baptist; some, Elijah; and others, Jeremiah, or one of the prophets." He said to them, "But who do you say that I am?" And Simon Peter answered, "Thou art the Christ, the Son of the living God." And Jesus said to him, "Blessed are you, Simon Bar-Jonah; for flesh and blood has not revealed this to you, but my Father who is in heaven. And I tell you, you are Peter, and upon this rock I will build my church; and the powers of death shall not prevail against it. I will give you the keys of the kingdom of heaven; and whatever you bind on earth shall be bound in heaven; and whatever you loose on earth shall be loosed in heaven."

CHRIST FORETELLS HIS DEATH AND RESURRECTION

From that time on Jesus began to tell his disciples how he must go to Jerusalem and suffer many things from the elders and chief priests and scribes, and be killed, and be raised again the third day. Then Peter took him, and began to rebuke him, saying, "Be it far from thee, Lord: this shall not happen to thee." But he turned and said to Peter, "Get behind me, Satan! You are a hindrance to me: for your thoughts are not God's thoughts, but the thoughts of men."

DISCIPLES ARE ALSO TO BEAR A CROSS

Great crowds followed him, and he turned and said to them, "If any man would come after me, let him deny himself, and take up his cross, and follow me. For whoever would save his life shall lose it; and whoever shall lose his life for my sake and the gospel's shall save it. For what will it profit a man, if he gains the whole world and forfeits his life? Or what shall a man give in exchange for his life?"

As he was going out on the road, a man came running up to him, and asked him, "Good Teacher, what shall I do that I may inherit eternal life?"

And Jesus said to him, "Why do you call me good? No one is good but God alone. You know the commandments, Do not kill, Do not commit adultery, Do not steal, Do not bear false witness, Do not defraud, Honor your father and mother." And he said to him, "Teacher, all these things have I observed from my youth." Then Jesus looking upon him loved him, and said, "One thing you lack; go, sell all that you have, and give it to the poor, and you will have treasure in heaven; and come, follow me."

But at these words his face fell, and he went away sorrowful: for he was one that had great possessions.

THE TRANSFIGURATION

After six days Jesus took Peter, James, and John his brother, and went up into a high mountain to pray.

As he prayed, he was transfigured before them, and his face shone as the sun, and his clothing became shining white like snow. And there appeared to them Moses and Elijah and they spoke of his approaching death at Jerusalem. As they departed from him, Peter said to Jesus, "Master, it is good for us to be here; and if thou wilt, let us make here three booths; one for thee, one for Moses, and one for Elijah." While he was still speaking, a bright cloud came over them; and a voice came out of the cloud, saying, "This is my beloved Son, in whom I am well pleased; listen to him."

When the disciples heard it, they fell on their faces and were filled with terror. But Jesus came and touched them, and said, "Arise and be not afraid." When they looked up, they saw no one but Jesus only.

"And there appeared to them Moses and Elijah"

GOING UP TO JERUSALEM

The disciples were on the road going up to Jerusalem, and Jesus was walking ahead of them; they were amazed and awe-struck; and those who followed did so in fear. Then once more calling to him the twelve, he began to tell them the things that were to happen to him, saying, "Behold, we are going up to Jerusalem; and the Son of Man shall be delivered to the chief priests and scribes; and they shall condemn him to death, and shall hand him over to the Gentiles: and they shall mock him, and shall spit upon him, and shall scourge him, and shall kill him; and after three days he shall rise again."

Then James and John, the sons of Zebedee, came up to him, saying, "Teacher, we would that thou do for us whatsoever we shall ask of thee." And he said to them, "What do you want me to do for you?" And they answered him, "Allow us to sit, one at thy right hand, and one at thy left hand, in thy glory." But Jesus said to them, "You do not know what you are asking. Are you able to drink the cup that I drink? or to be baptized with the baptism that I am baptized with?" And they said to him, "We are able."

Jesus said to them, "The cup that I drink, you shall drink; but to sit at my right hand or at my left hand is not mine to grant, but it is for them for whom it hath been prepared by my Father."

And when the ten heard it, they began to be indignant with James and John. But Jesus called them to him, and said, "You know that the rulers of the Gentiles lord it over them; and their great men exercise authority over them. But it shall not be so among you; but whoever would be great among you, shall be your servant; and whoever would be first among you,

shall be servant of all. For the Son of man also came not to be served, but to serve, and to give his life a ransom for many."

ZACCHAEUS

As Jesus was passing through Jericho, a man called Zacchaeus heard of his coming. Now Zacchaeus was the chief collector of taxes, and he was rich. He was anxious to see what sort of man Jesus was, but he could not because of the crowd, for he was short in stature. So he ran out in front, and climbed up into a sycomore tree to see him: for he was to pass that way.

And when Jesus came to the place, he looked up, and said to him, "Zacchaeus, make haste, and come down; for today I must stay at your house." And he made haste, and came down, and received him joyfully. And when the people saw all this, they began to complain, saying, "He has gone in to be the guest of a man who is a sinner." But Zacchaeus stood up, and said to the Lord, "Behold, Lord, the half of my property I give to the poor; and if I have wrongfully exacted money from any man, I repay him four times the amount."

And Jesus said to him, "Today salvation has come to this house, seeing that he also is a son of Abraham. For the Son of man came to seek and to save that which was lost."

THE RAISING OF LAZARUS

A certain man was sick, Lazarus of Bethany, of the village of Mary and her sister Martha. The sisters sent to him, saying, "Lord, behold, he whom thou lovest is sick." But when Jesus heard it, he said, "This sickness is not unto death, but for the glory of God, so that the Son of God may be glorified thereby."

Now Jesus loved Martha, and her sister, and Lazarus. So when he heard that he was sick, he remained two days longer in the place where he was. Then after this he said to the disciples, "Let us go into Judea again." The disciples said to him, "Rabbi, the Jews were but now seeking to stone thee: and goest thou thither again?" Jesus answered, "Are there not twelve hours in the day? If any man walks in the day, he does not stumble, because he sees the light of this world. But if a man walks in the night, he stumbles, because the light is not in him."

160

After this he said to them, "Our friend Lazarus has fallen asleep; but I go to awake him out of sleep." The disciples said to him, "Lord, if he has fallen asleep, he will recover." Now Jesus had spoken of his death, but they thought that he spoke of taking rest in sleep. Jesus therefore said to them plainly, "Lazarus is dead. And I am glad for your sakes that I was not there, so that you may believe. But let us go to him." Thomas, called the Twin, said to his fellow disciples, "Let us also go, that we may die with him."

When Jesus came, he found that Lazarus already had been in the tomb four days. Now Bethany was near Jerusalem, and many of the Jews had come to Martha and Mary, to console them over the loss of their brother. When Martha heard that Jesus was coming, she went and met him, but Mary still sat in the house. Martha said to Jesus, "Lord, if thou hadst been here, my brother would not have died. And even now I know that whatever thou shalt ask of God, God will give thee." Jesus said to her, "Your brother shall rise again." Martha answered, "I know that he shall rise again in the resurrection at the last day."

Jesus said to her, "I am the resurrection, and the life: he that believeth on me, though he die, yet shall he live; and whoever lives and believes on me shall never die. Do you believe this?" She said to him, "Yes, Lord: I have believed that thou art the Christ, the Son of God." And when she had said this she went away, and called Mary her sister, saying quietly, "The Teacher is here, and is calling for you."

And when she heard it, she rose quickly and went to meet him. (Now Jesus had not yet come into the village, but was still in the place where Martha had met him.) When the Jews who were with her in the house, consoling her, saw that Mary rose up quickly and went out, they followed her, supposing that she was going to the tomb to weep there. When Mary came where Jesus was, and saw him, she fell at his feet, saying, "Lord, if thou hadst been here, my brother would not have died."

When Jesus saw her weeping, and the Jews who came with her also weeping, he was deeply troubled, and said, "Where have you laid him?" They said to him, "Lord, come and see."

Jesus wept.

The Jews therefore said, "See how he loved him!" But some of them said, "Could not he, who opened the eyes of the blind man have kept this man from dying?" Then Jesus deeply moved again, came to the tomb. It was a cave, and a stone lay against it. Jesus said, "Take away the stone."

Martha, the sister of the dead man, said to him, "Lord, by this time there will be an odor, for he has been dead four days." Jesus said to her, "Did I not tell you that, if you would believe, you would see the glory of God?"

So they took away the stone.

And Jesus lifted up his eyes, and said, "Father, I thank thee that thou hast heard me. And I knew that thou hearest me always: but I have said this on account of the people standing by, that they may believe that thou didst send me." When he had said this, he cried with a loud voice, "Lazarus, come out!" He that was dead came out, his hands and feet bound with bandages, and his face wrapped with a cloth. Jesus said to them, "Unbind him, and let him go."

Many of the Jews therefore who came with Mary and saw what he did, believed in him. But some of them went away to the Pharisees, and told them what Jesus had done.

CHAPTER TEN

THE PASSION WEEK

THE TRIUMPHAL ENTRY INTO JERUSALEM

Not long after the raising of Lazarus Jesus and his disciples set out for Jerusalem.

As they came near the Mount of Olives, Jesus sent two of his disciples on ahead into the village. "As you enter, you will find tied there a colt that has never been ridden. Untie it and bring it here. And if anybody asks you 'Why are you doing this?' say, 'The Master has need of it, and will send it back here without delay'."

So they went and found a colt tied in the street as Jesus had said, and they untied it. Some of those who stood nearby asked, "What are you doing, untying the colt?"

But they answered as Jesus had told them to do, and the men let them take it. So they brought the colt to Jesus, and they threw their garments over it and Jesus mounted. Then many spread their garments on the road, and others leafy branches which they had cut in the fields, while those who led the way and those who followed, kept shouting,

"Hosanna! Blessed is he that cometh in the name of the Lord.
Hosanna in the highest."

JESUS WEEPS OVER JERUSALEM

As Jesus came into full view of the city, he wept aloud over it, saying, "If thou hadst known, even thou, the things which belong unto peace! but now they are hid from thine eyes. For the days shall come upon thee, when thine enemies shall cast up earthworks around thee and surround thee and shut thee in on all sides, and they will dash thee and thy children within thee to the ground; and they shall not leave in thee one stone upon another; because thou knewest not the time of thy visitation."

And he entered into the temple, and began to cast out those who were selling things there, saying, "It is written, and my house shall be a house of prayer, but you have made it a den of robbers."

The Triumphal Entry

164

When the chief priests and the scribes heard it, they sought how they might destroy him, for all the multitude was amazed at his teaching.

And every evening he and his disciples would leave the city.

CONSPIRACY AGAINST JESUS

When the feast of the Passover drew near, the chief priests and the scribes and the elders of the people assembled at the palace of Caiaphas, the high priest, and began to lay plans to arrest Jesus and kill him. But they decided not to do it on the feast day, lest there be an uproar among the people.

But Satan entered into Judas Iscariot, one of the twelve, and he went and spoke to the chief priest and his officers and asked, "What will you give me if I turn him over to you?"

When they heard this they were glad, and they agreed to pay him thirty pieces of silver. And from that time he was looking for an opportunity to betray him.

THE LAST SUPPER

And on the first day of unleavened bread, when they sacrificed the passover, his disciples said to him, "Where wilt thou that we go and make ready to eat the passover?" And he sent two of his disciples, and said to them, "Go into the city, and there shall meet you a man bearing a pitcher of water: follow him; and wheresoever he shall enter in, say to the master of the house, 'The Teacher saith, Where is my guest chamber, where I shall eat the passover with my disciples?' And he will himself show you a large upper room furnished and ready: and there make ready for us." And the disciples went to the city, and found as he had said to them: and they made ready the passover.

And at the evening he came with the twelve. And as they sat and were eating, Jesus said, "Verily I say unto you, One of you shall betray me, even he that eateth with me." They began to be sorrowful, and to say to him one by one, "Is it I?" And he said to them, "It is one of the twelve, he that dippeth with me in the dish. For the Son of man goeth, even as it is written of him: but woe unto that man through whom the Son of man is betrayed! Good were it for that man if he had not been born."

And as they were eating, he took bread, and when he had blessed, he brake it, and gave to them, and said, "Take, eat; this is my body." And he took

a cup, and when he had given thanks, he gave to them: and they all drank of it. And he said to them, "This is my blood of the covenant, which is poured out for many. Verily, I say unto you, I shall no more drink of the fruit of the vine, until that day when I drink it new in the kingdom of God."

JESUS WASHES THE DISCIPLES FEET

And during supper, the devil having already put into the heart of Judas Iscariot to betray him, Jesus, knowing that the Father had given all things into his hands, and that he came forth from God, and returned to God, rose from supper, and laid aside his garments; and he took a towel and girded himself. Then he poured water into the basin, and began to wash the disciples' feet, and to wipe them with the towel with which he was girded.

So he came to Simon Peter. He said to him, "Lord, dost thou wash my feet?" Jesus answered, "What I do thou knowest not now; but thou shalt understand hereafter." Peter said to him, "Thou shalt never wash my feet." Jesus answered him, "If I wash thee not, thou hast no part with me." Simon Peter said to him, "Lord, not my feet only, but also my hands and my head." Jesus said to him, "He who hath bathed needeth not to wash except for his feet, but is clean all over; and ye are clean, but not all." For he knew him that should betray him; therefore said he, "Ye are not all clean."

So when he had washed their feet, and taken his garments, and sat down again, he said to them, "Know ye what I have done to you? Ye call me, Teacher, and, Lord: and ye say well; for so I am. If I then, the Lord and the Teacher, have washed your feet, ye also ought to wash one another's feet. For I have given you an example, that ye also should do as I have done to you. Verily, verily, I say unto you, A servant is not greater than his lord; neither one that is sent greater than he that sent him. If ye know these things, blessed are ye if ye do them."

JUDAS ISCARIOT

When Jesus had said this, he was troubled in spirit, and said, "Verily, verily, I say unto you, that one of you shall betray me." The disciples looked at one another, doubting of whom he spoke. There was at the table reclining in Jesus' bosom one of his disciples, whom Jesus loved. Simon Peter therefore beckoned to him, and said to him, "Tell us who it is of whom he is speaking." He, leaning back, as he was, on Jesus' breast, said to him, "Lord, who is it?" Jesus answered, "He it is, for whom I shall dip the piece of bread, and give it him." So when he had dipped the piece of bread, he gave it to Judas Iscariot.

And after Judas had received the dipped piece of bread Satan entered into him. Jesus therefore said to him, "What thou doest, do quickly." Now no man at the table knew why he said this to him. For some thought, because Judas had the bag, that Jesus said to him, "Buy what things we need for the feast"; or, that he should give something to the poor. So Judas took the piece of bread and immediately went out. And it was night.

When he had gone out, Jesus said, "Now is the Son of man glorified, and God is glorified in him."

WORDS OF FAREWELL

Jesus said: "Let not your heart be troubled: believe in God, believe also in me. In my Father's house are many mansions; if it were not so, I would have told you; for I go to prepare a place for you. And if I go and prepare a place for you, I come again, and will receive you unto myself; that where I am, there ye may be also. And whither I go, ye know the way."

Thomas said to him, "Lord, we know not whither thou goest; how know we the way?" Jesus said to him, "I am the way, and the truth, and the life: no one cometh unto the Father, but by me.

"And whatsoever ye shall ask in my name, that will I do, that the Father may be glorified in the Son. If ye shall ask anything in my name, that will I do. If ye love me, ye will keep my commandments. And I will pray the Father, and he shall give you another Comforter, that he may be with you for ever, even the Spirit of truth: whom the world cannot receive; for it beholdeth him not, neither knoweth him, ye know him; for he abideth with you, and shall be in you. I will not leave you desolate: I come unto you.

"These things have I spoken unto you, while yet abiding with you. But the Comforter, even the Holy Spirit, whom the Father will send in my name, he shall teach you all things, and bring to your remembrance all that I said unto you.

"It is expedient for you that I go away; for if I go not away, the Comforter will not come unto you; but if I go, I will send him unto you. And he, when he is come, will convict the world in respect of sin, and of righteousness, and of judgment.

"I have yet many things to say unto you, but ye cannot bear them now. Howbeit when he, the Spirit of truth, is come, he shall guide you into all the truth: for he shall not speak from himself; but what things soever he shall hear, these shall he speak; and he shall declare unto you the things that are to come."

THE HIGH-PRIESTLY PRAYER

And lifting up his eyes to heaven, Jesus said: "Father, the hour is come; glorify thy Son, so the Son may glorify thee: even as thou gavest him authority over all flesh, that to all whom thou hast given him, he should give eternal life. And this is life eternal, that they should know thee the only true God, and him whom thou didst send, even Jesus Christ. I glorified thee on the earth, having accomplished the work which thou hast given me to do. And now, Father, glorify thou me with thine own self with the glory which I had with thee before the world was.

"I pray for them: I pray not for the world but for those whom thou hast given me; for they are thine; and all things that are mine are thine, and thine are mine: and I am glorified in them. I have given them thy word; and the world hated them, because they are not of the world, even as I am not of the world. I pray not that thou shouldst take them from the world, but that thou shouldst keep them from the evil one. They are not of the world, even as I am not of the world. Sanctify them in the truth: thy word is truth. As thou didst send me into the world, even so sent I them into the world. And for their sakes I sanctify myself that they themselves also may be sanctified in truth.

"Neither for these only do I pray, but for them also that believe on me through their word; that they may all be one; even as thou, Father, art in me, and I in thee, that they also may be in us: that the world may believe that thou didst send me. Father, I desire that they also whom thou hast given me be with me where I am, that they may behold my glory, which thou hast given me: for thou lovest me before the foundation of the world. O righteous Father, the world knew thee not, but I knew thee; and these knew that thou didst send me; and I made known unto them thy name, and will make it know; that the love wherewith thou lovest me may be in them, and I in them."

IN GETHSEMANE

When they had sung a hymn, they went out to the garden of Gethsemane, which was an enclosed place on Mount Olivet.

And Jesus said to his disciples, "All ye shall be offended: for it is written, 'I will smite the shepherd, and the sheep shall be scattered abroad.' But after I am raised up, I will go before you into Galilee." Peter said to him, "Although all shall be offended, yet will not I." And Jesus answered him, "Verily I say unto thee, that thou today, even this night, before the cock crow twice, shalt deny me thrice." But he spoke very vehemently, "If I must die with thee, I will not deny thee." And so said they all.

When they came to the garden Jesus said to the disciples, "Sit here while I pray."

Then he took with him Peter and James and John, and began to be full of sorrow and distress, and he said to them, "My soul is sorrowful unto death: stay here and watch."

Leaving the three apostles, he went forward a little distance, and falling on the ground, he prayed, "Abba, Father! If it is possible, let this cup pass from me; nevertheless, not as I will but as thou wilt." Then, rising, he came to the apostles, but they were asleep. "Could ye not watch for one hour? Watch and pray that ye enter not into temptation: the spirit indeed is willing, but the flesh is weak."

A View of the Garden of Gethsemane

And again he went away and prayed, saying the same words. And again he came and found them sleeping, and they did not know what to answer him.

For the third time he prayed in the same manner, saying the same words, and a great agony of distress having come upon him his sweat became like drops of blood falling to the ground.

When he rose from his prayer he came to his disciples and again found them sleeping. "Sleep on now," he said. "The hour has come. Behold, the Son of man is betrayed into the hands of sinners. Arise, let us be going. He that betrayeth me is at hand."

While he was still speaking, Judas came up, accompanied by a crowd of men armed with swords and clubs, sent by the high priests and elders of the people. Now the betrayer had agreed with them on a signal, saying, "The one whom I kiss is the man. Seize him!"

Judas went straight to Jesus and said, "Peace to thee, Master!" And he kissed him as if he loved him much.

Jesus said, "Friend, why have you come? Judas, dost thou betray the Son of man with a kiss?"

Then they arrested Jesus and led him away. And all the disciples left him and made their escape.

170

THE TRIAL BEFORE THE HIGH PRIEST

They led Jesus away to the high priest; and the chief priests and the elders and the scribes came together. And Peter had followed Jesus at a distance right into the courtyard of the high priest, and he sat down with the attendants and warmed himself in the light of the fire.

The chief priests and the whole council tried to get evidence against Jesus in order to put him to death; but they could find none, for while many gave false testimony against him, their evidence did not agree. Some got up and gave false witness against him saying, "We heard him say, I will destroy this temple that is made with hands, and in three days I will build another made without hands." And not even so did their evidence agree together.

And the high priest stood up and asked Jesus, saying, "Answerest thou nothing? What is it which these witness against thee?" But he held his peace, and answered nothing. Again the high priest asked him, and said to him, "Art thou the Christ, the Son of the Blessed?" And Jesus said, "I am: and ye shall see the Son of man sitting at the right hand of Power, and coming with the clouds of heaven." And the high priest tore his clothes, and said, "What further need have we of witnesses? Ye have heard the blasphemy: what think ye?" And they all condemned him to be worthy of death. And some began to spit on him, and to cover his face, and to strike him, and to say to him, "Now show us that you are a prophet!" And the officers struck him with their hands as they took charge of him.

PETER'S DENIAL

While Peter was down in the courtyard one of the maids of the high priest came up, and seeing Peter warming himself, she looked at him and said, "You also were with this Jesus of Nazareth."

But Peter denied it, saying, "I do not know what you, mean." Then he went out into the gateway, and the cock crowed.

The maid saw him in the gateway and began to tell those who stood by, "This man is one of them."

But he denied it again. And after a while those who stood there said to Peter, "You certainly are one of them, for you are from Galilee."

Then he began to curse and to swear, "I do not know this man that you are talking about." At that moment the cock crowed a second time.

And Peter remembered how Jesus had said to him, "Before the cock crows twice, thou shalt deny me thrice." And when he thought about it, he wept bitterly.

JESUS BEFORE PILATE

The next morning the great council of the Jews assembled and condemned Jesus to death. But since Judea was at that time under the government of Rome, the Jews were forbidden to inflict punishment of death on anyone until they had received permission from the Roman governor. They therefore took him before Pontius Pilate, who was the governor of Judea.

Pilate asked what was the accusation against Jesus. The crowd cried that he was a dangerous man, that he forbade the people to pay taxes to the Roman Emperor, and that he had declared himself to be Christ, the King.

Christ Before Pilate

(Artist: Munkacsy) John Wanamaker Photo

Then Pilate asked him, "Art thou the King of the Jews?" And he answered him, "Thou sayest." And the chief priests accused him of many things. And Pilate again asked him, saying, "Answereth thou nothing? behold how many things they accuse thee of." But Jesus made no further answer at all, so that Pilate marvelled.

Now at the feast he used to release for them one prisoner, whom they asked of him. And there was in prison a man called Barabbas, who had committed murder. A crowd went up and began to ask him for the usual favor. And Pilate answered them, "Shall I release for you the King of the Jews?" For he knew that the chief priests had handed him over on account of envy. But the chief priests stirred up the crowd, that he should rather release Barabbas. And Pilate again answered and said to them, "What then shall I do unto him whom ye call the King of the Jews?" And they cried out again, "Crucify him." And Pilate said to them, "Why, what evil hath he done?" But they shouted all the louder, "Crucify him." And Pilate, wishing to satisfy the multitude, released to them Barabbas, and delivered Jesus, when he had scourged him, to be crucified.

And the soldiers led him away inside the courtyard, called the Praetorium; and they brought together the whole battalion. And they dressed him up in a purple cloak and making a crown of thorns, they put it on him; and they began to salute him, "Hail, King of the Jews!" They struck him on the head with a stick and spat upon him, and bowing their knees they did homage to him. When they had mocked him, they took off from him the purple robe and put his own clothes on him. Then they took him out of the city to crucify him.

THE CRUCIFIXION

As they came out of the city they stopped a passer-by, Simon of Cyrene, coming from the country, and laid the cross on him to carry after Jesus.

He was followed by a large multitude of people and also of women who beat their breasts and wept aloud in their sorrow over him; but Jesus turned to them and said, "Daughters of Jerusalem, weep not for me, but weep for yourselves and for your children!"

And they brought him to Golgotha, which means The Place of the Skull. And they offered him drugged wine, but he would not take it. Then they crucified him. And Jesus said, *"Father forgive them; for they know not what they do."*

It was nine o'clock in the morning when they crucified him. And they set up over his head a written notice of the charge against him, saying in both Hebrew and in Latin and in Greek: THIS IS JESUS THE KING OF THE JEWS. And when they had crucified him they divided up his garments among them, casting lots to decide what each should take.

With him they crucified two robbers; one on his right hand, and one on his left. And they that passed by jeered at him, wagging their heads, and saying, "Ha! thou that destroyest the temple, and buildest it in three days, save thyself, and come down from the cross." The chief priests also made sport of him among themselves and the scribes said, "He saved others; himself he cannot save. Let the Christ, the King of Israel, now come down from the cross, that we may see and believe."

And one of the malefactors that were hanged railed on him, saying, "Art not thou the Christ? Save thyself and us." But the other answered, and rebuking him said, "Dost thou not even fear God, seeing thou art in the same condemnation? And we indeed justly; for we receive the due reward of our deeds: but this man hath done nothing amiss." And he said, "Jesus, remember me when thou comest in thy kingdom." And he said to him, *"Verily I say unto thee, Today shalt thou be with me in Paradise."*

By the cross of Jesus the mother of Jesus was standing, and his mother's sister, Mary the wife of Clopas, and Mary Magdalene. When Jesus saw his mother, and his favorite disciple standing near, he said to his mother, *"Woman, behold thy son!"* Then he said to the disciple, "Behold thy mother!" And from that hour John took her to his home to care for her as if she were his own mother.

At noon darkness spread over the whole land and lasted until three in the afternoon. Then Jesus cried with a loud voice, "Eloi, Eloi, lama sabachtani?" which means, *"My God, my God, why hast thou forsaken me?"*

And some of those who stood there, when they heard it, said, "He is calling Elijah."

174

The Crucifixion

After this Jesus, knowing that all things are now finished, that the scripture might be accomplished, said, *"I thirst."* There was set there a vessel full of sour wine, so they put a sponge full of the sour wine upon hyssop, and held it to his mouth.

When Jesus therefore had received the wine, he said, *"It is finished."*

And crying with a loud voice, he said, *"Father, into thy hands I commend my spirit;"* and having said this, he bowed his head and gave up his spirit.

And the veil of the temple was rent in two from the top to the bottom. When the centurion, who stood facing him, saw how he breathed his last, he said, "Truly this man was the Son of God." And there were also women watching from a distance: among whom were both Mary Magdalene and Mary the mother of James the younger and of Joses, and Salome; who, when he was in Galilee, followed him, and waited on him; and many other women that came up to Jerusalem with him.

175

THE BURIAL

Toward evening, as it was the Preparation—that is, the day preceding the Sabbath—there came a rich man from Arimathea, named Joseph. He was a respected member of the great council, who was himself living in expectation of the kingdom of God. He summoned up courage to go to Pilate and ask for the body of Jesus. Pilate could hardly believe that he was already dead, and he sent for the captain of the guard to find out whether he was dead yet, and when he learned from the captain that he was, he gave Joseph permission to take the body.

Then Joseph brought a linen sheet and took him down and wrapped him in the linen sheet, and laid him in a tomb that had been hewn out of a rock, and rolled a stone against the entrance to the tomb. And Mary Magdalene and Mary the mother of Joses were looking on and saw where he was put.

CHAPTER ELEVEN

THE RESURRECTION AND THE ASCENSION

EASTER MORNING

When the Sabbath was past, Mary Magdalene, and Mary the mother of James, and Salome, bought spices to anoint the body of Jesus. And very early on the first day of the week, they came to the tomb, and they were saying among themselves, "Who shall roll away the stone for us from the entrance to the tomb?" And looking up, they saw that the stone was already rolled back; for there had been a great earthquake and an angel of the Lord had descended from heaven and rolled away the stone.

Entering into the tomb, they saw a young man sitting on the right side, clothed in a white robe; and they were terrified. And he said to them, "Be not afraid; you are looking for Jesus, the Nazarene, who has been crucified. He is risen; he is not here: this is the place where they laid him! But go, tell his disciples and Peter that he is going before you into Galilee: there you shall see him, as he told you." So they came out, and fled from the tomb; for trembling and astonishment had come upon them. And they hurried to bring the news to the disciples.

When Peter and John heard the report, they ran to the tomb. John outran Peter, but Peter went into the tomb first, followed by the younger disciple. Both saw the empty tomb and believed.

THE JOURNEY TO EMMAUS

On that same day two of the disciples were walking to Emmaus, a village about seven miles from Jerusalem, and were talking about these events. In the midst of their conversation Jesus came and joined them, though they were prevented from recognizing him.

"What is this you are talking about so earnestly?" he asked them.

They stood still, looking sad. One of them, named Cleopas, answered, "Are you a stranger lodging alone in Jerusalem, seeing that you do not know what has happened these past days?"

"What things?" asked the Master.

"All about Jesus of Nazareth," they said. And they told him of the mighty works of Jesus and how the rulers had put him to death. "But we hoped

"He is risen"

COPR. BY PROVIDENCE LITHOGRAPH CO.

*"Jesus came
and joined them"*

that it was he that would redeem Israel," they added, and then went on to tell of the strange report that he had risen from the dead.

Jesus answered them, "O foolish men, and slow to believe what the prophets have spoken! Was it not necessary for Christ thus to suffer and then enter into his glory?"

And beginning with Moses and the prophets, he explained to them the passages in Scriptures concerning himself.

When they came near to the village to which they were going, he made as if he were going further. But they urged him to remain with them. "Abide with us," they said, "for it is toward evening, and the day is now far spent."

So he went in to stay with them. But as soon as he sat down with them and had taken the bread and had blessed and broken it, and was handing it to them, their eyes were opened and they knew it was the Lord. At that moment he vanished out of their sight.

"Were not our hearts burning within us while he talked to us and explained the Scriptures to us?" they said one to the other. Then they rose up and returned to Jerusalem and found the eleven and the rest gathered together.

"Yes, it is true," they said, "the Master is risen indeed, and has appeared to Simon."

DOUBTING THOMAS

In the evening of that day, the first day of the week, when the doors were shut where the disciples were, for fear of the Jews, Jesus came and stood in their midst, and said to them, "Peace be unto you." And when he had said this, he showed them his hands and his side. The disciples were filled with joy when they saw the Lord.

But Thomas, one of the twelve, called Didymus, was not with them when Jesus came. The other disciples therefore said to him, "We have seen the Lord." But he said, "Except I shall see in his hands the print of the nails, and put my finger into the print of the nails, and put my hand into his side, I will not believe."

A week later his disciples were again in the house, and Thomas was with them. Jesus came, the doors being shut, and stood in their midst, and said, "Peace be unto you." Then he said to Thomas, "Reach hither thy finger, and see my hands; and reach hither thy hand, and put it into my side: and be not faithless, but believing." Thomas answered and said to him, "My Lord and my God!" Jesus said to him, "Because thou hast seen me, thou hast believed: blessed are they that have not seen, and yet have believed."

AT THE SEA OF GALILEE

After these things Jesus appeared again to the disciples at the sea of Tiberias. There was Simon Peter, and Thomas called Didymus, and Nathaniel of Cana in Galilee, and the sons of Zebedee, and two other disciples.

Simon Peter said to them, "I am going fishing." They said, "We will go with you." So they went into the boat; and that night they caught nothing. But when day was dawning, Jesus stood on the beach, though the disciples did not know it was Jesus.

Jesus said to them, "Boys, have you anything to eat?" They answered him, "No." And he said to them, "Cast the net on the right side of the boat, and you will find fish." So they threw the net in, and now they were not able to draw it for the quantity of fish. That disciple therefore whom Jesus loved said to Peter, "It is the Lord." So when Simon Peter heard that it was the Lord, he put on clothes (for he was naked), and plunged into the water. But the other disciples came in the little boat (for they were not far from the land, but about three hundred yards), dragging the net full of fish.

When they got out upon the land, they saw a fire of coals there, and fish broiling on it, and bread. Jesus said to them, "Bring some of the fish that you have caught." Simon Peter therefore went up, and drew the net to land, full of great fishes, a hundred and fifty and three: and although there were so many, the net was not torn. Jesus said to them, "Come to breakfast." And none of the disciples dared ask him who he was, for they felt sure that it was the Lord. Jesus came and took the bread, and gave them some, and the fish likewise. This is now the third time that Jesus was manifested to the disciples, after he had risen from the dead.

When they had broken their fast, Jesus said to Simon Peter, "Simon, son of John, lovest thou me more than these?" He said to him, "Yea, Lord; thou knowest that I love thee." He said to him, "Feed my lambs." He said to him again a second time, "Simon, son of John, lovest thou me?" He said to him, "Yea, Lord; thou knowest that I love thee." He said to him, "Tend my sheep." He said to him the third time, "Simon, son of John, lovest thou me?" Peter was grieved because he said to him the third time, "Lovest thou me?" And he answered, "Lord, thou knowest all things; thou knowest that I love thee." Jesus said to him, "Feed my sheep."

THE GREAT COMMISSION

The eleven disciples went into Galilee, to the mountain where Jesus had arranged to meet them. And when they saw him, they worshipped him. Yet some doubted. Jesus, however, came near to them and said to them, "All authority hath been given unto me in heaven and on earth. Go ye therefore, and make disciples of all the nations, baptizing them into the name of the Father and of the Son and of the Holy Spirit: teaching them to observe all things whatsoever I commanded you: and lo, I am with you always, even unto the end of the world."

THE ASCENSION

And he led them out until they were near Bethany: and he lifted up his hands, and blessed them. And it came to pass, while he was blessing them, he parted from them, and was carried up into heaven. They worshipped him, and returned to Jerusalem with great joy. Afterwards they were continually in the temple, blessing God.

And they went forth, and preached everywhere, the Lord working with them, and confirming the word by the signs that followed.

WHY THE GOSPEL WAS WRITTEN

Jesus did many other signs in the presence of the disciples which are not written in this book: but these are written, that ye may believe that Jesus is the Christ, the Son of God; and that believing ye may have life in his name.

"It is the Lord"

182

CHAPTER TWELVE

THE BEGINNING OF THE CHRISTIAN CHURCH

THE ASCENSION

Saint Luke has written the story of the beginning of the Christian Church. In our Bible, this story is called the Acts of the Apostles. It covers a period of about thirty years.

Luke's account begins with the story of the ascension of our Lord.

Jesus charged the disciples not to depart from Jerusalem, but to wait for the promise of the Father. "John indeed baptized with water; but ye shall be baptized in the Holy Spirit not many days hence."

When they had come together, they asked him, saying, "Lord, dost thou at this time restore the kingdom to Israel?" And he said to them, "It is not for you to know times or seasons, which the Father hath set within his own authority. But ye shall receive power, when the Holy Spirit is come upon you: and ye shall be my witnesses both in Jerusalem, and in all Judea and Samaria, and unto the uttermost part of the earth."

And when he had said these things, as they were looking, he was taken up; and a cloud received him out of their sight. And while they were looking steadfastly into heaven as he went, behold two men stood by them in white apparel. They said, "Men of Galilee, why do you stand looking into heaven? This Jesus, who was taken up from you into heaven, will so come in the same way as you saw him go into heaven."

Then they returned to Jerusalem from the mount called Olivet, which is near Jerusalem. And they went up to the upper room, where they were staying; Peter and John and James and Andrew, Philip and Thomas, Bartholomew and Matthew, James the son of Alphaeus, and Simon the Zealot, and Judas the son of James. All these with one accord continued in prayer, together with the women and Mary the mother of Jesus, and with his brothers.

PENTECOST

After the Ascension, the Apostles and a number of others who had followed Jesus met every day for prayer, and they spent much time in the temple, praising God. At one of their meetings they chose Matthias as an apostle to take the place of Judas Iscariot.

And when the day of Pentecost (fifty days after Easter) had come, they were all together in one place. And suddenly there came from heaven a sound as of the rushing of a mighty wind, and it filled all the house where they were sitting. And there appeared to them tongues that looked like fire. And they were all filled with the Holy Spirit, and began to speak with other tongues, as the Spirit gave them words to say.

Now there were dwelling at Jerusalem Jews, devout men from every nation under heaven. And when this sound was heard, the multitude came together, and were amazed because every man heard them speaking in his own language. And they were excited with wonder, saying, "Behold, are not all these that speak Galilaeans? And how is it that we hear, each of us in his own native language, about the mighty works of God?"

And they were all amazed and perplexed, saying one to another, "What does this mean?" But others mocking said, "They are filled with new wine."

But Peter, standing up with the eleven, lifted up his voice and spoke to them, saying, "Men of Judaea and all who dwell in Jerusalem, let this be known to you, and give ear to my words. For these men are not drunk, as you suppose since it is only the third hour of the day; but this is what was spoken through the prophet Joel:

And in the last days it shall be, declares God,
That I will pour out my Spirit upon all flesh,
And your sons and your daughters shall prophesy,
And your young men shall see visions,
And your old men shall dream dreams;
And it shall be that whoever calls on the name of the Lord shall
    be saved.

Men of Israel, hear these words: Jesus of Nazareth, a man approved of God by mighty works and wonders and signs which God did by him in your midst, as you yourselves know—this Jesus, delivered up according to the definite plan and foreknowledge of God, you crucified and killed by the hands of lawless men. But God raised him up, having loosed the pangs of death, because it was not possible for him to be held by it.

This Jesus did God raise up, and of that we all are witnesses. Being therefore exalted by the right hand of God, and having received from the Father the promise of the Holy Spirit, he has poured out this which you see and hear. Let all the house of Israel therefore know assuredly, that God has made him both Lord and Christ, this Jesus whom you crucified."

When they heard this, they were cut to the heart, and said to Peter and the rest of the apostles, "Brethren, what shall we do?" And Peter said to them, "Repent, and be baptized every one of you in the name of Jesus Christ for the forgiveness of your sins; and you shall receive the gift of the Holy Spirit. For the promise is to you and to your children, and to all that are far off, every one whom the Lord our God calls to him."

And he testified with many other words and exhorted them, saying, "Save yourselves from this crooked generation." Then those who received his word were baptized, and there were added that day about three thousand souls. And they continued steadfastly in the apostles' teaching and fellowship, in the breaking of bread and in prayers.

THE CHURCH AT JERUSALEM

Those who believed the gospel and joined the church shared everything that they had with one another. They even sold their property and divided the money with all the rest. Every day, attending the temple together and breaking bread together in their homes, they ate their food with glad and generous hearts, praising God and having favor with all the people. And every day the Lord added to the church those who were being saved.

Soon, however, a persecution arose. The mighty works done by the apostles and their preaching about Jesus aroused the anger of the high priests and the Sadducees. So the apostles were commanded not to preach any more or even to teach in the name of Jesus. But the apostles answered, "We must obey God rather than men."

Finally Peter and John were arrested and beaten. But even this harsh treatment did not stop the apostles from telling others the story of Jesus; rather, they rejoiced that they were counted worthy to suffer for his name. And many more, both men and women, joined the band of believers.

When the number of the disciples was multiplying, there arose a complaint of the Grecian Jews against the Hebrews, because their widows were neglected in the daily ministration. And the twelve called the multitude of the disciples, and said, "It is not fitting that we should forsake the word of God, to serve tables. Look ye out therefore, brethren, from among you seven men of good report, full of the Spirit and of wisdom, whom we may appoint to undertake the duty. But we will continue steadfastly in prayer, and in the ministry of the word."

And the saying pleased the whole multitude, and they chose seven men, whom they brought before the apostles: and when they had prayed, they laid their hands upon them in blessing.

STEPHEN

One of these seven deacons, Stephen, did great wonders among the people. But certain Jews arose to dispute with him. But they were not able to withstand the wisdom and the Spirit with which he spoke. So they hired men to testify falsely against him and stirred up the people, and the elders, and the scribes. And they seized him and brought him to the council for trial, setting up false witnesses who said, "This man does not stop speaking words against this holy place, and the law: for we have heard him say that this Jesus of Nazareth shall destroy this place, and shall change the customs which Moses delivered to us." And all who sat in the council, fastening their eyes on him, saw his face like the face of an angel.

Then Stephen answered for himself and spoke of the things which the God of Abraham and Isaac and Jacob had done to their fathers and how their fathers had always resisted the will of God and how they themselves had hardened their hearts until they murdered Jesus Christ.

When they heard these things, they were cut to the heart and they gnashed their teeth at him. But he, being full of the Holy Spirit, looked up steadfastly into heaven, and saw the glory of God, and Jesus standing on the right hand of God, and said, "Behold, I see the heavens opened, and the Son of man standing on the right hand of God." But they cried out with a loud voice, and stopped their ears, and rushed upon him; and they dragged him out of the city, and stoned him, and the witnesses laid down their garments at the feet of a young man named Saul. And they stoned Stephen, who called upon the Lord, saying, "Lord Jesus, receive my spirit." And he kneeled down, and cried with a loud voice, "Lord, lay not this sin to their charge." And when he had said this, he fell asleep.

And Saul fully approved of his death.

THE GOSPEL IN SAMARIA

And Philip went down to the city of Samaria, and preached to them the gospel of Christ. The multitudes gave heed with one accord to the things that were spoken by Philip, when they heard him and saw the signs which he did. And there was great joy in that city. When they believed, they were baptized, both men and women. When the apostles who were in Jerusalem heard that Samaria had received the word of God, they sent Peter and John to continue the work among them.

THE DARK-SKINNED MAN FROM ETHIOPIA

A man of Ethiopia, an officer of great authority under Candace, queen of the Ethiopians, had come to worship at Jerusalem. He was returning, in his chariot, and was reading Isaiah, the prophet (53.7-8). Then the Spirit said to Philip, "Go near, and join this chariot." And Philip heard him read and said, "Do you understand what you are reading?" He said, "How can I, unless some one guides me." And he invited Philip to come up and sit with him. Then Philip, beginning with the message of Isaiah, the prophet, told him the good news of Jesus. And as they went along the road they came to some water, and the Ethiopian said, "See, here is water; what is to prevent my being baptized?" And he commanded the chariot to stop; and they went down into the water, and Philip baptized him. And the dark-skinned officer went on his way rejoicing.

COPR. BY PROVIDENCE LITHOGRAPH CO.

THE CONVERSION OF SAUL

After the martyrdom of Stephen, Saul became one of the most active persecutors of the Christians. Determined to put a stop to their preaching, he went to the high priest in Jerusalem and secured letters to the authorities in Damascus, giving him power to arrest every man or woman whom he would find either believing in Jesus or teaching in his name.

So he started for Damascus. On the way a bright light flashed round him. Struck as if by lightning, he fell to the ground and heard a voice saying, "Saul, Saul, why dost thou persecute me?" Saul asked who spoke to him, and the voice said, "I am Jesus, whom thou persecutest. But rise, and go into the city, and it shall be told thee what thou must do."

Meanwhile the men who traveled with Saul were standing speechless with amazement, hearing the voice, but seeing no one. When he rose from the ground, he discovered that he could not see. His companion led him into Damascus, and till the third day he remained without sight, and did not eat or drink anything.

In this city lived a man named Ananias. The Lord commanded him to go to Saul and place his hands upon him. But Ananias hesitated to go. "I have heard how much evil he has done to the Christians at Jerusalem," he said. But the Lord answered, "Go thy way: for he is a chosen vessel to bear my name to the Gentiles and kings, and the children of Israel."

So Ananias went. No sooner had he touched Saul than the converted man could see. Saul rose and was baptized. His name was changed to Paul.

With the zeal of a new convert, Paul began to preach Jesus. And all that heard it were astonished. The Jews became very angry and in many ways plotted to put him to death, but God protected him.

So the church throughout all Judea and Galilee had peace and was built up; and walking in the fear of the Lord and the comfort of the Holy Spirit, the church increased in numbers.

CORNELIUS

At Caesarea lived a man named Cornelius. He was a Roman army officer in command of a company of soldiers. He was religious and God-fearing, and so were all the members of his household. He was also liberal in his gifts to charity, and continually offered prayer to God.

One afternoon, while he was at prayer, an angel appeared to him and told him to send to Joppa for a man named Peter, who would tell him what to do. Cornelius sent two soldiers and a God-fearing servant at once.

About the time the messengers drew near to Joppa, Peter was praying; he also had a vision. In this vision God made it clear to him that the gift of salvation was not for Jews only, but was also for the Gentiles.

While Peter was thinking of the meaning of this vision, the men sent by Cornelius came to the house where he was staying and asked for him. They told him of the request of their master, so Peter went with them to the home of Cornelius.

Cornelius had invited all his kinsman and intimate friends to be present. When Peter went in, he said to them, "You know that a Jew is forbidden to associate with a Gentile or visit him; but God has taught me that in the sight of God there is no distinction between Jews and Gentiles, and that Christ has died for all men." So Peter told Cornelius and the people assembled at his house of the saving power of Jesus Christ. And the people believed this gospel and were baptized.

THE FIRST CHURCH AMONG THE GENTILES

Those who were scattered by the persecution that arose when Stephen was stoned, traveled about, preaching the word of God. At first they told the story of Jesus only to the Jews. But some who went to a city called Antioch preached also to Gentiles, telling them of the Lord Jesus. And a great number believed and turned to the Lord.

When news of these things came to the church in Jerusalem, they sent Barnabas to Antioch to advise the converts in that city. After visiting Antioch, Barnabas went to Tarsus to find Paul and bring him to Antioch. For a whole year they met with the church and taught many people. It was in this city of Antioch that the disciples of Christ were first called Christians.

RENEWAL OF PERSECUTION

After the conversion of Cornelius, Peter returned to Jerusalem.

About the year 44, Herod Agrippa, the king, again began a persecution of the Christians. He beheaded James the brother of John, and when he saw that this pleased the Jews, he put Peter in prison.

COPR. BY PROVIDENCE LITHOGRAPH CO.

"The men sent by Cornelius came to the house where Peter was staying"

The Christians prayed earnestly for Peter. The night before he was to have been brought out for punishment Peter lay bound in chains between two soldiers, while guards walked before the door.

Suddenly an angel stood before him, and a light shone in the cell. The angel touched Peter and bade him rise and put on his clothes. The chains fell from his hands, and Peter obeyed, not knowing whether or not it was a vision he saw. They passed the first and second guard, and came to an iron gate that of itself opened for them. After they had passed out into the city the angel left him. Then Peter came to himself and saw that God had sent an angel to set him free.

In the morning there was a great stir among the soldiers. No one could tell how Peter had escaped or where he had gone. Herod questioned the soldiers and then punished them severely.

PAUL'S FIRST MISSIONARY JOURNEY

After his conversion, Paul was received with much joy among many of the followers of Jesus. A few, however, were suspicious of him because he had been such a bitter enemy. For some time he continued to teach at Antioch, but after a while he and Barnabas were sent to preach to the Gentiles.

Being guided by the Holy Spirit, they sailed to the island of Cyprus. Here they proclaimed the word of God in the synagogues of the Jews. John Mark assisted them. Among those who came to believe was Sergius, the governor of Cyprus.

From Cyprus, Paul and his companions sailed to Perga in Asia Minor. Here John Mark left them and returned to Jerusalem.

Going from Perga, they went to Antioch in Pisidia. Here they preached to both Jews and Gentiles. Many were converted, but some of the Jews were filled with jealousy and grew very much excited. Coming together, they opposed Paul. Then he told them, "It was our duty to preach to you first; now you have rejected the word of God, and we are turning to the Gentiles."

The word of the Lord was spread throughout the region, but the Jews continued to cause trouble for Paul and Barnabas and drove them away. However, they went on to other cities, preaching the gospel and establishing churches. It seemed that nothing could stop them.

At Lystra Paul healed a man who had been lame from birth. When the people saw this, they thought Paul and Barnabas were gods, and wished to offer sacrifice to them, but Paul forbade it. Many came to believe.

But soon Jews came from the cities where the apostles had been preaching and they succeeded in stirring up persecution against them. A mob formed and stoned Paul. Then they dragged him out of the city, and left him, thinking that he was dead. But Paul recovered and returned to the city. The next day he and Barnabas went on to Derbe. When they had preached the gospel in that city, and had made many disciples, they returned to Antioch, passing through the places where they had already preached. Everywhere they encouraged believers to remain faithful, and in every church they appointed elders to be leaders.

Upon their return to Antioch, the city from which they had started their journey, they called the church together and reported all the things that God had done with them and that he had opened a door of faith to the Gentiles.

PAUL'S SECOND MISSIONARY JOURNEY

After having remained for a time in Antioch, Paul and Barnabas were sent to Jerusalem to explain to the leaders there about the work among the Gentiles. Upon their return to Antioch these two men were ready to set out upon a second missionary journey. Barnabas wanted to take John Mark with them, but Paul objected, feeling that the young man who had deserted them on the first journey would not be much help to them. The result was that Paul and Barnabas separated. Barnabas took John Mark with him and

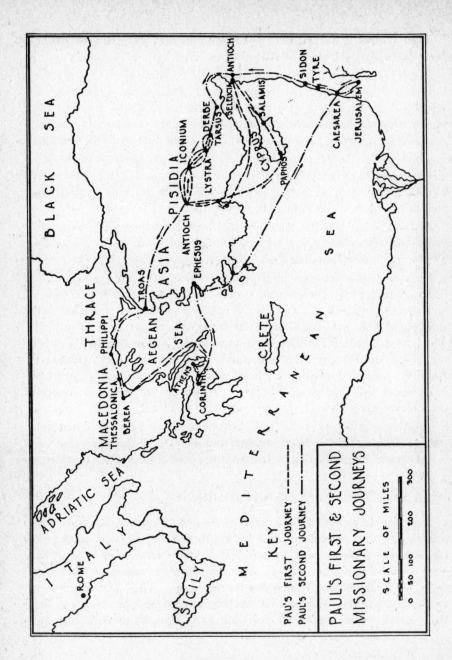

BLACK SEA

THRACE

MACEDONIA

PHILIPPI

THESSALONICA

BEREA

ATHENS

CORINTH

AEGEAN SEA

TROAS

ASIA

PISIDIA

ANTIOCH

EPHESUS

ICONIUM

DERBE

LYSTRA

TARSUS

SELEUCIA

ANTIOCH

CYPRUS

SALAMIS

PAPHOS

SIDON

TYRE

CAESAREA

JERUSALEM

CRETE

MEDITERRANEAN SEA

ADRIATIC SEA

ITALY

ROME

SICILY

KEY

PAUL'S FIRST JOURNEY
PAUL'S SECOND JOURNEY

PAUL'S FIRST & SECOND
MISSIONARY JOURNEYS

SCALE OF MILES

0   50 100   200   300

sailed again for Cyprus. Paul took with him a good man by the name of Silas, and they journeyed westward and northward through Syria and Cilicia, visiting some of the churches established during the first missionary tour.

On this second journey Paul found a young disciple, named Timothy, whom he took with him. And they went northward and eastward until they came to Troas. Here Paul had a vision. During the night a man of Macedonia stood before him and said, "Come over into Macedonia and help us." From this Paul understood that the Lord had called them to preach the gospel in Europe. So they sailed over to Macedonia, taking Luke the physician with them. This same Luke later wrote the Gospel according to Luke as well as the Acts of the Apostles.

In Macedonia they visited several cities, including Philippi and Thessalonica. Then Paul went southward into Greece. He made a brief stay in Athens, after which he went on to Corinth. Here Paul remained a year and a half, preaching the word of God. And many Corinthians believed and were baptized.

Afterwards Paul returned to Asia Minor, stopping for a while in the city of Ephesus. From there he crossed the Mediterranean to Jerusalem, where he visited the church and told them how the Gentiles were believing the gospel and becoming Christians. After that he returned to Antioch, the city from which he had started.

PAUL'S THIRD MISSIONARY JOURNEY

After spending some time at Antioch, Paul set out on his third missionary journey. He went over all the country of Galatia and Phrygia, instructing and encouraging the believers, and came to Ephesus. Here he remained for about three years, making his home with Priscilla and Aquila. He worked for a living making tents and spent most of his spare time preaching the gospel and encouraging believers. And the word of God grew mightily and many believed, so that sorcery and idolatry were checked in many parts of western Asia Minor.

Paul then crossed over to Macedonia to visit other churches that he had founded, and he spent three months in Corinth. After that he went to Jerusalem, bringing with him a collection from the churches to the poor Christians in Jerusalem.

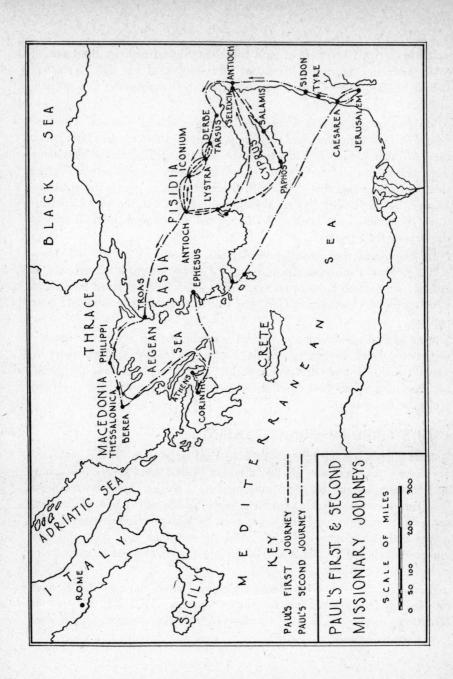

PAUL'S FIRST & SECOND
MISSIONARY JOURNEYS

KEY

PAUL'S FIRST JOURNEY ———————
PAUL'S SECOND JOURNEY —·—·—·—

SCALE OF MILES

0 50 100   200   300

Paul the Apostle

PAUL ARRESTED AND IMPRISONED

When Paul arrived in Jerusalem, the Christians received him gladly. And when he told them what things God had done among the Gentiles by his ministry, they thanked God.

James, one of the leaders of the church at Jerusalem, suggested to Paul that, in order to show his loyalty to the laws of Moses, he should take part in a series of Jewish ceremonies in the temple with four other men. This Paul agreed to do, though the request really was unreasonable.

The conversion of Paul had been a sore blow to the Jews who refused to believe on Christ. Then one day, when some of the Jews from Asia Minor saw Paul in the temple, they excited a mob against him. In order to save him from being killed it became necessary for the Roman soldiers to rescue him and take him to jail.

Then Paul was given an opportunity to speak for himself. He told the people of his conversion and of the command God had given him to preach the gospel to the Gentiles.

But the crowd shouted against him so much that the chief officer ordered that he should be flogged. Then, when they had tied him, Paul asked the captain that stood by, "Does the law permit you to flog a Roman citizen, especially one who has not been found guilty of any wrong?"

The captain hurried to tell the chief officer, and the chief officer came at once and asked him, "Are you a Roman citizen?" "Yes," answered Paul. "I paid a great price for my citizenship," said the chief officer. "But I was born a free Roman," answered Paul.

So the men who were about to torture him immediately left him, and the chief officer was afraid when he knew that he had bound a Roman citizen and had just been ready to have him flogged.

The next day the officer had Paul brought before the chief priests and council of the Jews. But the council could not agree. Some favored releasing him. Others insisted on punishing him. Finally there arose a great dissension, and the Roman captain, fearing that Paul would be pulled to pieces, commanded the soldiers to take him by force from them, and bring him into the castle. Then some of the Jews plotted to storm the castle and kill Paul, but Paul's sister's son heard of the plan and told it to the Roman officer.

That night the officer sent Paul, guarded by more than four hundred men, on his way to Caesarea, a city almost a hundred miles away. Here he was safe from the mob and here he was to be tried by Felix, the governor.

Paul remained in prison for two long years. Finally he gave up hope of ever getting a fair trial in Caesarea, so he decided to appeal to the emperor at Rome. This he had a right to do, since he was a Roman citizen.

After a troublesome voyage, Paul, accompanied by Luke, arrived at Rome. Here he was allowed to live in a house that he rented, though he was constantly guarded by a soldier. For two years he lived this way, and many people came to hear him preach and teach the things that belong to the kingdom of God. No one hindered him, and Paul, though a prisoner, continued to work as a missionary.

LETTERS TO THE CHURCHES

Paul not only preached the gospel and founded churches, but he also gave much attention to caring for the churches among the Gentiles. For this reason he wrote many letters while on his journeys as well as during his imprisonment. In these letters or *epistles,* as they are called, he explained the most important teachings of the Christian religion and gave needed advice about the affairs of the churches. At least a dozen of these letters, some of which were written to churches, others to individuals, are preserved in the New Testament. Paul's writing of letters did much to strengthen and encourage the scattered Christians who either read his messages or heard them read as they gathered for meetings in synagogues and homes.

The following Epistles were written by Paul, either while he was on one of his missionary journeys or during his imprisonment:

Romans	Philippians	1 Timothy
1 Corinthians	Colossians	2 Timothy
2 Corinthians	1 Thessalonians	Titus
Galatians	2 Thessalonians	Philemon
Ephesians		

THE TEACHINGS OF PAUL

Paul was a great man of action. He traveled far on the sea and on the great military roads of the Roman Empire, bringing the good news of salvation to many people. He reached most of the great cities of the then civilized

*Reading a Letter
from Paul to One
of the Churches*

COPR. BY PROVIDENCE LITHOGRAPH CO.

world. Like a bold explorer or a powerful conqueror, he established many outposts for the kingdom of God.

But Paul was also a great teacher. More than any other follower of Christ he has helped people to understand the glorious meaning of the gospel. Many good books have been written to explain the teachings of Paul, but in a brief Bible history we must limit ourselves to focusing attention on what is most outstanding. In the message of this great servant of God there are three facts that are very important for us to keep in mind.

First, he set forth with great interest and understanding *the doctrine of justification by faith.* How does a sinner get right with God? All of us are sinners. No human being has ever lived who has not sinned against God; the only exception is Jesus Christ, who was tempted in all things just as we are, but without sin. Each of us is accountable to God for all that he has done. We cannot hide from Him. God will not be deceived.

How are we to get right with him? By being religious? By being better than other people? By praying, making sacrifices, keeping certain days holy, doing for others? No! None of these things can make us acceptable to God. The only way we can have peace with him is through trusting in his love and mercy. We cannot save ourselves, but God can save us, and he desires to do it. For Jesus Christ has redeemed us, bought and freed us from all sins, from death, and from the power of the devil; not with silver and gold, but with his holy and precious blood and his innocent sufferings and death. God asks us to believe this good news, and to take him at his word. Believing

198

this, we have peace with God. We are counted righteous and acceptable to God because Jesus Christ has been obedient for us and he has suffered the penalty of our sin for us. We are made right with God when we commit ourselves completely into His keeping.

This is the great doctrine of justification by faith.

Second, Paul taught that salvation is for all people. He had been brought up to think that God cared only for the Jews. After his conversion he came to see that God would have all men to be saved and come to the knowledge of the truth. Jesus had made this plain when he lived on this earth, but not even all of the Twelve understood it. Paul was the first Christian missionary to the Gentiles, and it is largely because of his zeal for the spread of the gospel that we in America today have been brought up in the Christian faith.

Third, Paul gave much attention to the practical application of Christianity. While it is true that we are made right with God, not by our good works, but by faith in the grace of Christ alone, it is also true that Christian faith never stands alone. If a person is united with Christ as a believer and disciple, he will strive to do good and to avoid all evil. Christianity has to do with the way we live. As Paul said, in his letter to the Galatians: "I have been crucified with Christ; and it is no longer I that live, but Christ liveth in me: and that life which I now live I live in faith, the faith which is in the Son of God, who loved me, and gave himself up for me."

The Gentiles who were converted to Christ through Paul's missionary work had been brought up in an atmosphere of paganism. They had been worshippers in the temples of heathen gods, and their standards of right and wrong were different from those of the Christian faith. These people knew practically nothing of the Old Testament, the Ten Commandments, and the long history of faith in the one God which had preceded the coming of Christ. The position of women and children and of slaves was very pitiable. Worldliness, moral corruption, ignorance and superstition were widespread.

It was one of the greatest tasks of history when Paul undertook to bring these Gentile converts into the knowledge and practice of Christianity. After he founded a church in a city and filled it with enthusiasm, he would go on to a new field. Often, however, he found, to his sorrow, that after he had gone the enthusiasm died down; the Gentiles, many of them, slipped back to their old pagan practices, strife broke out between factions, and the life of the soul was being choked by selfishness, lust, laziness, or the worship of false gods. So Paul would write to rebuke his converts for their mistakes and instruct them in the way that was right. At times, after taking his friends to task, he would break out in a strain of beautiful eloquence, writing with poetic fervor some of the finest things in all literature, as for example, his beautiful and very wise words about Christian love in the Thirteenth Chapter of the First Epistle to the Corinthians.

PAUL'S LAST DAYS

Tradition says that after two years of imprisonment in Rome Paul was set free. What happened to him after that is not told us in the Bible. However, there is a tradition that he undertook a fourth missionary journey to parts of Asia Minor, Macedonia, and possibly also to Spain.

During this time the emperor Nero began to persecute the Christians. Finally Paul was seized and imprisoned again. But this time he was not treated with the same kindness. Many Christians suffered martyrdom by being thrown to the lions in the great coliseum at Rome. Paul, however, was put to death by being beheaded, since this kind of death was considered less disgraceful for a Roman citizen.

Shortly before his death Paul wrote a farewell letter to Timothy, the young man who had proved to be a loyal friend and faithful helper. We

might expect it to be a sad letter, but it was not, for Paul was cheerful and hopeful. He was sure of victory through Christ. In closing, he said,

"The time of my departure has come. I have fought the good fight, I have finished the course, I have kept the faith: henceforth there is laid up for me the crown of righteousness, which the Lord, the righteous judge, shall give to me at that day; and not only to me, but also to all them that have loved his appearing."

200

THE OTHER APOSTLES

Peter

Peter, James (the son of Zebedee) and John, who had been the most devoted disciples of Jesus, became the chief leaders of the Christian church among the Jews.

After spending several years in Jerusalem, Peter journeyed about as a bearer of the gospel message, especially to the Jews who were scattered in the cities of Asia Minor and southern Europe.

There are several stories about the later life of Peter, but they are not in the Bible and we cannot be sure that they are true. The Bible, however, does show that Peter traveled about as a missionary, that his wife went with him at least a part of the time, and that at times Mark accompanied him as a co-worker and interpreter. There are also two short epistles in the New Testament that bear his name.

These letters were written to give hope and courage to Christian believers who were being persecuted for their religion, and also to help them to see that by living lives of purity and goodness they were to overcome the hatred and slanders of their enemies.

The story is told that in the course of his missionary journeys Peter finally reached the city of Rome. Here a persecution broke out against the Christians. Peter was taken prisoner and sentenced to be crucified, as the Christ whom he followed had been before him. Then Peter, so the story goes, begged to be crucified head downward, humbly saying that he was not worthy to die in the same manner as his Master had died.

James and John

James, the son of Zebedee, was beheaded in Jerusalem when Herod began to persecute the Christians, and he thus became the first of the apostles to suffer martyrdom.

John, his brother, who is spoken of as "the disciples whom Jesus loved," labored at first together with Peter in Palestine. During the later years of his life he ministered to churches in Asia Minor. John lived to a great age. There are five books in the New Testament that are generally regarded as

"The Gospel was brought to many nations"

having been written by him: the Gospel according to John, the three Epistles of John, and Revelation.

Matthew

Matthew, sometimes called Levi, spent many years in preaching the gospel, especially in Judea. Though most of his own Jewish race had despised him for becoming a follower of Jesus, he still wanted to work among them and have them know Jesus as he knew him and be happy as he was happy.

Matthew wrote the gospel that bears his name. It was written particularly for Jewish people, to show them that Jesus was the promised Messiah, who had come to fulfill teachings of the law and the prophets and to save his people from their sins.

Nothing is known for sure of Matthew's last years. Tradition says, however, that after working faithfully among his own people in Judea for about fifteen years, he went to spread the gospel in foreign lands. One story reports that he went to Ethiopia, in northeastern Africa.

James and Judas

James, the Lord's brother, became the leader of the church at Jerusalem after the departure of Peter and the death of James, the son of Zebedee. He was considered one of the pillars of the church, along with Peter and John. The Epistle of James is thought to have been written by him, although some scholars think that the author was another person.

Another of the apostles was Judas (not Iscariot), also called Thaddaeus. Nothing is known of his later life, but there is a tradition that he went as a missionary to Mesopotamia.

The Co-workers of Paul

Among the co-workers with Paul the most prominent were: Timothy, Luke, Barnabas, John Mark, Titus, Silas, and Apollos.

Timothy accompanied Paul on his second and third missionary journeys and proved to be a very faithful friend and true servant of the Lord. Paul affectionately referred to him as "Timothy, my son." The older apostle put

Timothy in charge of the church in Ephesus and to that place he sent him two epistles.

Luke was a physician by training. He joined Paul and his party on the second missionary journey and was with him a great part of the time from then until Paul's death. He wrote the Gospel that bears his name, addressing it chiefly to Gentiles and showing that Jesus is the merciful Saviour of all men. Luke also wrote the Acts of the Apostles, in which he has given us a record of how the gospel of Jesus was spread from Jerusalem to most parts of the Roman Empire.

"FOR THE GRACE OF GOD has appeared for the salvation of all men, training us to renounce irreligion and worldly passions, and to live sober, upright lives in this world, awaiting our blessed hope, the appearing of the glory of our great God and Saviour Jesus Christ, who gave himself for us to redeem us from all iniquity and to purify for himself a people of his own who are zealous for good deeds."

Titus 2. 11-14

A CHRONOLOGICAL
SURVEY

A KEY TO
PRONUNCIATION

A CHRONOLOGICAL SURVEY

We are not certain of all the dates listed below. Not all scholars are agreed, for example, as to the year when Jesus was born. It is known, however, that Jesus was born before the death of Herod I, which took place in the year 4 B.C. Since Jesus was but an infant when Joseph and Mary took him to Egypt, we conclude that he was born perhaps the very year of Herod's death. The list given below is intended chiefly for the purpose of showing the general relationship and order of events.

POLITICAL HISTORY   SACRED HISTORY

Rome	Palestine	
44 B.C. Julius Caesar murdered.		
31 B.C. Caesar Augustus Emperor.	37 B.C. Herod I made king.	4 B.C. John the Baptist born.
	4 B.C. Death of Herod the Great.	4 B.C. Jesus born.
	Kingdom divided between sons of Herod.	
	To Archelaus: Judea, Samaria, Idumea.	
	To Herod Philip: Territory e a s t of Galilee.	
	To Herod Antipas: Galilee and Perea.	
14 A.D. Tiberius Emperor.	6 A.D. Archelaus removed from office. Judea and Samaria governed by a Roman procurator.	26 A.D. Ministry of John the Baptist.
		29 A.D. Death of John the Baptist.
	25 A.D. Pontius Pilate procurator.	30 A.D. The Passion, Death and Resurrection of Jesus.
		33 A.D. Stoning of Stephen.
		Conversion of Saul.

Rome	Palestine	
37 A.D. Gaius Emperor.	37 A.D. Herod Agrippa I receives territory of Philip and title of king.	
	39 A.D. Herod Antipas deposed and his territory added to that of Agrippa.	
41 A.D. Claudius Emperor.	41 A.D. Judea also given to Agrippa. All Palestine again under a Herodian prince.	
	44 A.D. Herod Agrippa I dies. All Palestine under a Roman procurator responsible to the governor of Syria.	44 A.D. James martyred.
		46-49 A.D. Paul's first missionary journey.
		49-52 A.D. Paul's second missionary journey.
		52-58 A.D. Paul's third missionary journey.
54 A.D. Nero Emperor.	53 A.D. Herod Agrippa II appointed ruler of tetrarchy of Philip and parts of Galilee and Perea.	58-60 A.D. Paul a prisoner in Caesarea.
		60-61 A.D. Paul's voyage to Rome.
64 A.D. Great fire in Rome. Persecution of Christians by Roman Government begun.		61-63 A.D. Paul a prisoner in Rome.
		63-66 A.D. Paul's later journeys.
	66 A.D. Rebellion of Jewish zealots.	66 A.D. Second arrest.
68 A.D. Galba Emperor.		67 A.D. Execution of Paul.
69 A.D. Vespasian Emperor.		67 A.D. Crucifixion of Peter.
69 A.D. Titus sent with army to restore order in Palestine.	70 A.D. Destruction of Jerusalem.	70 A.D. Destruction of Jerusalem.

A KEY TO PRONUNCIATION OF PROPER NAMES

ā	as in	fāme	ê	"	êvent	oo	"	food
ă	"	ăm	ī	"	īce	ū	"	ūse
ȧ	"	sofȧ	ĭ	"	ĭf	ŭ	"	ŭs
ä	"	ärm	ō	"	ōld	iȧ	as	yah
â	"	senâte	ŏ	"	ŏdd	iah	"	yah
ē	"	ēve	ŏ	"	ōbey	ian	"	yan
ĕ	"	ĕnd	ô	"	ôrb	ion	"	yun
ē	"	makēr						

A
Abel, ā'bel
Abijah, a-bī'jah
Absalom, ăb'sa-lom
Agrippa, a-grĭp'ȧ
Ahab, ā'hăb
Alphaeus, ăl-phē'us
Amalek, ăm'a-lĕk
Amaziah, ăm-a-zī'ah
Amos, ā'mos
Antioch, ăn'ti-ŏk
Antipas, ăn'ti-păs
Apollos, a-pŏl'os
Aquila, ăk'wĭ-lȧ
Ararat, ăr'a-răt
Archelaus, är-ke-lā'us
Artaxerxes, är-tax-ērx'ēz
Ashdodites, ăsh'dod-īts
Asher, ăsh'er
Assyria, a-sĭr'i-ȧ
Athens, ăth'enz
Augustus, ô-gŭs'tus

B
Baal, bā'al
Babel, bā'bel
Babylon, băb'ĭ-lon
Babylonia, băb-ĭ-lō'ni-a
Barabbas, bär-ăb'as
Barnabas, bär'na-bas
Bartholomew, bär-thŏl'o-mū
Bartimaeus, bär'ti-mā'us
Bath-sheba, băth-shē'ba

Bethany, bĕth'a-nĭ
Bethlehem, bĕth'le-hem
Bethphage, bĕth'pha-jê
Bildad, bĭl'dăd
Blastus, blăs'tus
Boaz, bō'az

C
Caesar, sē'zar
Caesarea Philippi, ses-a-rē'ȧ phĭ-lĭp'ī
Cain, kān
Caiphas, kā'ia-phas
Cana, kā'na
Canaan, kā'naan
Canaanite, kā'naan-īt
Capernaum, ka-pēr'na-um
Centurion, sĕn-tū'rĭ-ŭn
Cephas, sē-phas
Chaldeans, kăl-dē'ans
Chebar, kē'bar
Cherith, kē'rith
Chronicles, krŏn'i-kls
Cilicia, sĭ-lĭ'siȧ
Cleopas, klē'o-pas
Clopas, klō'pas
Colossae, ko-lŏs'ê
Colossians, kō-lŏs'sians
Corinth, kŏr'inth
Corinthians, ko-rĭn'thi-ans
Cornelius, kor-nē'li-us
Cyprus, sī'prus
Cyrene, sī-rē'nê

209

D Damascus, da-măs′kus
Darius, da-rī′us
Delaiah, dĕl-a-ī′ah
Derbe, dĕr′be

E Eden, ē′den
Edom, ē′dom
Eli, ē′lī
Eli, eli, lama sabachtani,
  ē′lī, ē′lī, lā′ma sā-băk-tā′nī
Elijah, ē-lī′jah
Eliphaz, ĕl′i-phaz
Elisabeth, e-lĭz′a-bĕth
Elisha, ē-lī′shà
Elkanah, ĕl′kă-nah
Emmaus, em-mā′us
Ephesians, e-phē′sians
Ephesus, ĕph′e-sus
Esau, ē′sô
Esdraelon, ĕs-dra-ē′lon
Ethiopia, ē-thi-ō′pi-a
Euphrates, ū-phrā′tēz
Exodus, ĕx′ō-dŭs

G Gabriel, gā′bri-el
Gad, găd
Galatia, ga-lā′tià
Galatians, ga-lā′tianz
Galilee, găl′i-lee
Gamaliel, ga-mā′li-el
Gaza, gā′zà
Gedaliah, gĕd-a-lī′ah
Genesis, jĕn′ê-sis
Gennesaret, gen-nĕs′a-ret
Gethsemane, gĕth-sĕm′a-ne
Gideon, gĭd′ê-on
Gilead, gĭl′ê-ad
Goliath, go-lī′ath
Gomorrah, go-mŏr′ah
Goshen, gō′shen

H Haggai, hăg′ga-ī
Ham, hăm
Haran, hā′ran
Hebron, hē′bron
Herod, hĕr′od
Herodias, he-rō′di-as
Hivite, hī′vīt
Hosanna, hō-zăn′à
Hosea, hō-zē′a
Hoshea, hŏ-shē′a

I Iconium, ī-kō′ni-um
Isaac, ī′zaak
Isaiah, ī-zā′iah
Iscariot, ĭs-kăr′i-ot
Ishmaelites, ĭsh′ma-el-īts
Israel, ĭz′ra-el
Issachar, ĭs′sa-kar

J Jairus, ja-ī′rus
Japheth, jā′pheth
Jehovah, jê-hō′vah
Jeremiah, jĕr-e-mī′ah
Jericho, jĕr′ĭ-kō
Jeroboam, jĕr-o-bō′am
Jerusalem, je-roo′sa-lĕm
Jeshua, jĕsh′u-a
Jesse, jĕs′sê
Jesus, jē′zŭs
Joab, jō′ăb
Joash, jō′ăsh
Job, jōb
Johannan, jō-hā′nan
Jonah, jō′nah
Joppa, jŏp′pà
Josephus, jō-sē′fus
Joshua, jŏsh′u-à
Josiah, jō-sī′ah

Judea, jū-dē'à
Jupiter, jū'pĭt-er

O Omri, ŏm'rī
Onesimus, o-nĕs'i-mus

K Kidron, kĭd'ron

P Palestine, păl'es-tīne
Pamphylia, pam-phĭl'i-à
Passover, păss'ō-ver
Pentecost, pĕn'tê-cost
Perea, pē-rē'à
Perga, pēr'gà
Persians, pēr'zi-ans
Pharaoh, phā'rōh, phā'râ-ō
Pharisees, phăr'i-sēz
Philemon, phī-lē'mon
Philippi, phĭ-lĭp'ī
Philistines, phĭ-lĭs'tĭnz
Phrygia, frĭj'i-à
Pisidia, pī-sĭd'i-à
Pontius Pilate, pŏn'shĭ-us, pŏn-shŭs, pŏn'tĭ-ŭs pī'lât
Potiphar, pŏt'i-phēr
Priscilla, prĭ-sĭl'là
Procurator, prŏk'u-rā-tēr

L Laban, lā'ban
Lazarus, lăz'a-rŭs
Lebanon, lĕb'a-non
Levi, lē'vī
Lot, lŏt
Lycaonia, lĭk'â-ō'ni-à
Lystra, lĭs'trà

M Macedonia, măs-e-dō'ni-à
Magdalene, măg'dà-lĕn
Mammon, măm'on
Medes, mēdz
Mercury, mer'kūr-ĭ
Mesopotamia, mĕs-o-po-tā'mi-a
Messiah, mě-sī'àh
Micah, mī'kà
Midianites, mĭd'i-an-īts
Moses, mō'zĕz

R Rabbah, răb'bah
Rachel, rā'chel
Rebekah, rē-bĕk'ah
Rehoboam, rē-ho-bō'am

N Naamathite, nā'a-ma-thīt
Nain, nā'in
Naomi, nā-ō'mī
Naphtali, năph'ta-lī
Nathanael, na-thăn'a-el
Nazareth, năz'a-rĕth
Nebuchadnezzar, nĕb-u-kad-nĕz'zar
Nehemiah, nē-he-mī'ah
Nero, nē'rō
Nicodemus, nik-o-dē'mus
Nineveh, nĭn'e-veh

S Sadducees, săd'du-sēz
Samaria, sa-mā'ri-à
Samaritan, sa-măr'i-tan
Sarah, sā'rah
Shalmaneser, shăl-man-ē'zēr
Shaphat, shā'phat
Shem, shĕm
Shemer, shē'mer

Shuhite, shoo'hīt
Sidon, sī'don
Silas, sī'las
Simeon, sĭm'e-on
Simon, sī'mon
Sinai, sī'nī', sī'nâ-ī
Sodom, sŏd'om
Solomon, sŏl'o-mon
Synagogue, sĭn'a-gŏg
Syria, sĭr'i-å

T Tarshish, tär'shish
Tarsus, tär'sus
Temanite, tē'man-īt
Thessalonians, thĕ-sa-lō'ni-ans
Thessalonica, thĕs-sa-lo-nī'kå
Timothy, tĭm'o-thĭ

Titus, tī'tus
Tyre, tīr

U Uriah, u-rī'ah
Uzziah, uz-zī'ah

Z Zacchaeus, ză-kē'us
Zacharias, zăk-a-rī'as
Zealot, zĕl'ŭt
Zebedee, zĕb'e-dē
Zebulun, zĕb'u-lŭn
Zechariah, zĕk-a-rī'ah
Zedekiah, zĕd-e-kī'ah
Zerubbabel, ze-rŭb'ba-bĕl
Zipporah, zĭ-pō'rah
Zoar, zō'ar
Zobah, zō'bah
Zophar, zō'phar